With the compliments

of

NATHAN AZIZOLLAHOFF
Oriental Carpets & Textiles

OCC - Top Floor, Building A,

105 Eade Road, London N4 1TJ
Tel.(0)181 802 0077 Fax.(0)181 802 1144
E-mail: nathan.co@ndirect.co.uk

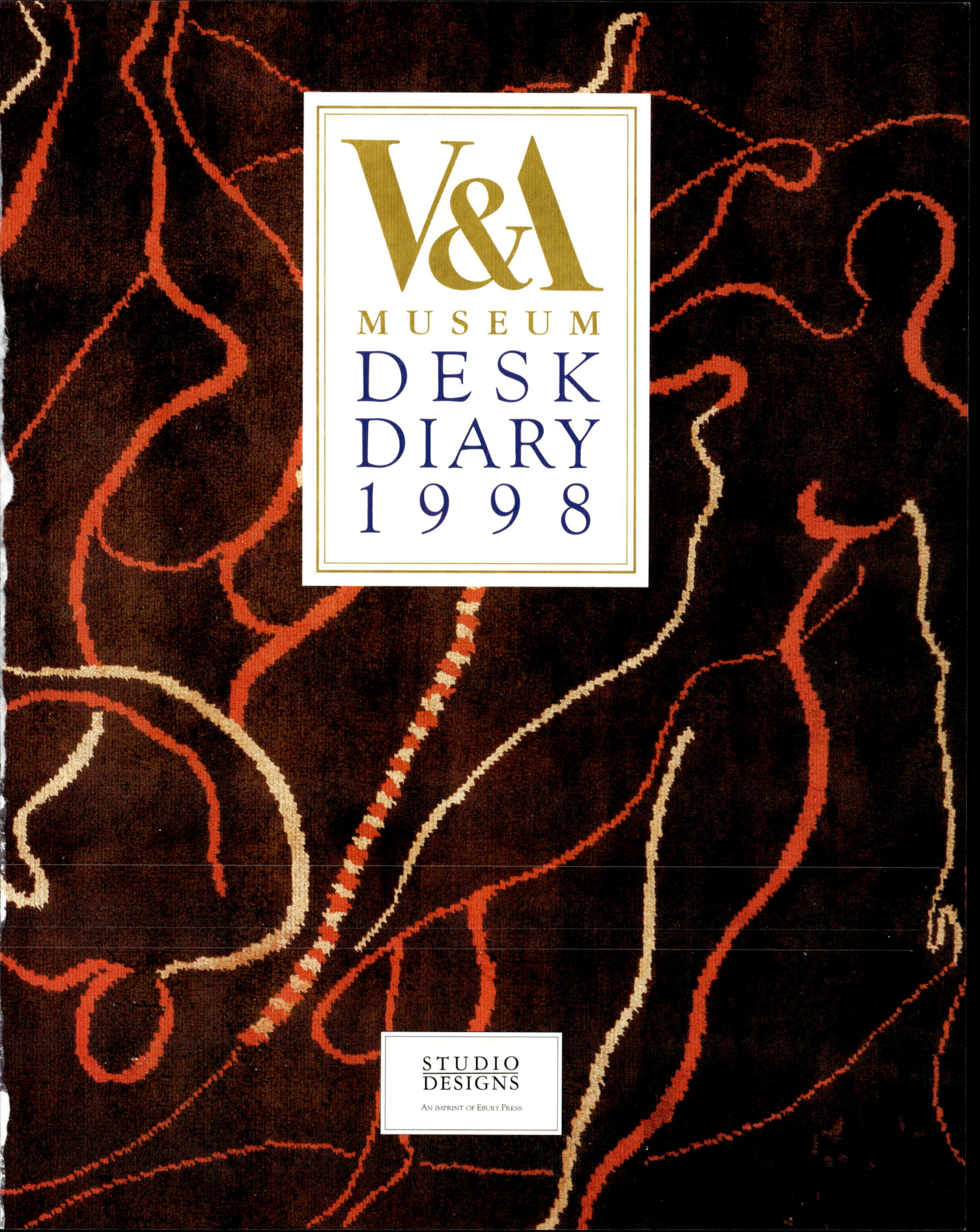

First published in the United Kingdom in 1997 by Studio Designs
An imprint of Ebury Press,
Random House, 20 Vauxhall Bridge Road, London SW1V 2SA

Random House UK Limited Reg. No. 954009

Copyright © Random House UK Ltd 1997
Illustrations, introduction and captions © Board of Trustees, Victoria & Albert Museum, London 1997

Licensed by V&A Enterprises Limited.

All rights reserved. No part of this book may be reproduced in any form or by any means without permission in writing from the publisher.

Whilst every effort has been made to ensure accuracy, the publishers cannot accept liability for errors.

Warning: Clauses in the Banking and Financial Dealings Act allow the Government to alter dates at short notice. The Clearing Banks in Scotland will now follow UK bank holidays unless indicated otherwise.

Calendarial and Astronomical data included in this diary is reproduced with permission, from data supplied by HM Nautical Almanac Office © Copyright Particle Physics and Astronomy Research Council.

Set in Goudy by M.A.T.S.

Printed and bound in Singapore
Designed by David Fordham

ISBN 0 09 185272 2

PERSONAL DETAILS

NAME	TELEPHONE (HOME)	DRIVING LICENCE NO.
ADDRESS	TELEPHONE (BUSINESS)	BANK SORT CODE
	NATIONAL INSURANCE NO.	BANK A/C NO.
	PASSPORT NO.	

The V&A Patrons offer the Museum's highest level of corporate and private support. For information, please contact
The Development Office on 0171 938 8271
For information on joining the Friends of the V&A contact the Friends Office on 0171 938 8472
MUSEUM HOURS OF OPENING
Monday 12 noon – 17.50   Tuesday – Sunday 10.00 – 17.50
Closed Christmas Eve, Christmas Day, Boxing Day and New Year's Day

Front cover: Detail from a pair of 19th century Persian saddle bags, woven with coloured wools in reverse soumak.
T306-1910

1998 YEAR PLANNER

JANUARY
M	T	W	T	F	S	S
			1	2	3	4
5	6	7	8	9	10	11
12	13	14	15	16	17	18
19	20	21	22	23	24	25
26	27	28	29	30	31	

FEBRUARY
M	T	W	T	F	S	S
						1
2	3	4	5	6	7	8
9	10	11	12	13	14	15
16	17	18	19	20	21	22
23	24	25	26	27	28	

MARCH
M	T	W	T	F	S	S
30	31					1
2	3	4	5	6	7	8
9	10	11	12	13	14	15
16	17	18	19	20	21	22
23	24	25	26	27	28	29

APRIL
M	T	W	T	F	S	S
		1	2	3	4	5
6	7	8	9	10	11	12
13	14	15	16	17	18	19
20	21	22	23	24	25	26
27	28	29	30			

MAY
M	T	W	T	F	S	S
				1	2	3
4	5	6	7	8	9	10
11	12	13	14	15	16	17
18	19	20	21	22	23	24
25	26	27	28	29	30	31

JUNE
M	T	W	T	F	S	S
1	2	3	4	5	6	7
8	9	10	11	12	13	14
15	16	17	18	19	20	21
22	23	24	25	26	27	28
29	30					

JULY
M	T	W	T	F	S	S
		1	2	3	4	5
6	7	8	9	10	11	12
13	14	15	16	17	18	19
20	21	22	23	24	25	26
27	28	29	30	31		

AUGUST
M	T	W	T	F	S	S
31					1	2
3	4	5	6	7	8	9
10	11	12	13	14	15	16
17	18	19	20	21	22	23
24	25	26	27	28	29	30

SEPTEMBER
M	T	W	T	F	S	S
	1	2	3	4	5	6
7	8	9	10	11	12	13
14	15	16	17	18	19	20
21	22	23	24	25	26	27
28	29	30				

OCTOBER
M	T	W	T	F	S	S
			1	2	3	4
5	6	7	8	9	10	11
12	13	14	15	16	17	18
19	20	21	22	23	24	25
26	27	28	29	30	31	

NOVEMBER
M	T	W	T	F	S	S
30						1
2	3	4	5	6	7	8
9	10	11	12	13	14	15
16	17	18	19	20	21	22
23	24	25	26	27	28	29

DECEMBER
M	T	W	T	F	S	S
	1	2	3	4	5	6
7	8	9	10	11	12	13
14	15	16	17	18	19	20
21	22	23	24	25	26	27
28	29	30	31			

1999 YEAR PLANNER

JANUARY
M	T	W	T	F	S	S
				1	2	3
4	5	6	7	8	9	10
11	12	13	14	15	16	17
18	19	20	21	22	23	24
25	26	27	28	29	30	31

FEBRUARY
M	T	W	T	F	S	S
1	2	3	4	5	6	7
8	9	10	11	12	13	14
15	16	17	18	19	20	21
22	23	24	25	26	27	28

MARCH
M	T	W	T	F	S	S
1	2	3	4	5	6	7
8	9	10	11	12	13	14
15	16	17	18	19	20	21
22	23	24	25	26	27	28
29	30	31				

APRIL
M	T	W	T	F	S	S
			1	2	3	4
5	6	7	8	9	10	11
12	13	14	15	16	17	18
19	20	21	22	23	24	25
26	27	28	29	30		

MAY
M	T	W	T	F	S	S
31					1	2
3	4	5	6	7	8	9
10	11	12	13	14	15	16
17	18	19	20	21	22	23
24	25	26	27	28	29	30

JUNE
M	T	W	T	F	S	S
	1	2	3	4	5	6
7	8	9	10	11	12	13
14	15	16	17	18	19	20
21	22	23	24	25	26	27
28	29	30				

JULY
M	T	W	T	F	S	S
			1	2	3	4
5	6	7	8	9	10	11
12	13	14	15	16	17	18
19	20	21	22	23	24	25
26	27	28	29	30	31	

AUGUST
M	T	W	T	F	S	S
30	31					1
2	3	4	5	6	7	8
9	10	11	12	13	14	15
16	17	18	19	20	21	22
23	24	25	26	27	28	29

SEPTEMBER
M	T	W	T	F	S	S
		1	2	3	4	5
6	7	8	9	10	11	12
13	14	15	16	17	18	19
20	21	22	23	24	25	26
27	28	29	30			

OCTOBER
M	T	W	T	F	S	S
				1	2	3
4	5	6	7	8	9	10
11	12	13	14	15	16	17
18	19	20	21	22	23	24
25	26	27	28	29	30	31

NOVEMBER
M	T	W	T	F	S	S
1	2	3	4	5	6	7
8	9	10	11	12	13	14
15	16	17	18	19	20	21
22	23	24	25	26	27	28
29	30					

DECEMBER
M	T	W	T	F	S	S
		1	2	3	4	5
6	7	8	9	10	11	12
13	14	15	16	17	18	19
20	21	22	23	24	25	26
27	28	29	30	31		

Introduction

THE VICTORIA & ALBERT MUSEUM has one of the world's largest and most representative collections of carpets, with almost 1,400 pieces equally divided into European and non-European carpets.

It has taken 150 years to assemble this collection and it continues to grow; the collecting policy still largely determined by that formulated when the Museum was first established in the 1850s. As the Museum of Manufacturers (the name was changed to the Victoria & Albert Museum in 1899), objects were collected in order to demonstrate principles of good design to students, designers, manufacturers and consumers.

In the middle of the 19th century, carpet manufacturers in Britain tended to use designs typical of the Victorian's love of nature in all its exuberance. Detailed, naturalistic blossoms were woven in great abundance – often interspersed with architectural elements such as 'gothic' ruins or fanciful, oriental pavilions. These designs might have made attractive pictures, but the sense of perspective they conveyed could be disturbing on a carpet. In line with many art historians, the Museum authorities considered that three-dimensional images conflicted with the essential flatness of carpets.

Carpets with geometric patterns were thus selected by the Museum to illustrate how good and functional designs should be used. Floral patterns, especially those on Persian carpets, were not totally ignored; in contrast to British designers, the work of 'oriental' artists was considered to be distinguished by an intuitive understanding of the correct principles of design. These design skills can be clearly seen in two important 16th-century Persian carpets: the Chelsea Carpet and the Ardabil Carpet. When recommending that the Museum should purchase the Ardabil Carpet, William Morris wrote that its 'design is of singular perfection...and therefore most especially valuable for a museum, the special aim of which is the education of the public in Art'.

JENNIFER WEARDEN
Assistant Curator Textiles and Dress
Victoria and Albert Museum

Page 1: Detail of acrobats from a hand-knotted carpet designed by V. Boberman for the Maison de Décoration Intérieure Moderne in Paris c. 1929.

T.366-1977

Opposite: A brightly coloured carpet woven by the Qashqai people of south-eastern Iran in the 1920s or 1930s.

T.9-1945

December 1997– January 1998

WEEK 1

MONDAY
29

TUESDAY
30

WEDNESDAY
31
                                                                                                                    First day of Ramadan

THURSDAY
1
                                                                                                                    Holiday, New Year's Day

T	F	S	S	M	T	W	T	F	S	S	M	T	W		T	F	S	S	M	T	W	T	F	S	S	M	T	W
18	19	20	21	22	23	24	25	26	27	28	29	30	31		1	2	3	4	5	6	7	8	9	10	11	12	13	14

December 1997 – January 1998

Holiday, Scotland (tbc)

FRIDAY
2

SATURDAY
3

SUNDAY
4

The village women with their work-calloused fingers made four carpets a year, three for sale and one for the household . . . the women rose at 4.30am daily and knotted for 14 hours, pausing only for scant meals and strictly timed tea-breaks.

From an interview, 'Carpet Magic', by Veronica Horwell in *The Times*, 26 June 1983.

Overleaf: Detail from a silk tapestry-woven carpet which is Turkish and dates from the 19th century. Carpets woven using this technique are often called kelims and, because they are not very sturdy; one as fine as this would probably have been used as a decorative cover or hanging.

T.107-1962

January

WEEK 2

MONDAY
5

◐

TUESDAY
6

Epiphany   Holiday, Italy

WEDNESDAY
7

THURSDAY
8

T	F	S	S	M	T	W	T	F	S	S	M	T	W	T	F	S	S	M	T	W	T	F	S	S	M	T	W	T	F	S
1	2	3	4	5	6	7	8	9	10	11	12	13	14	15	16	17	18	19	20	21	22	23	24	25	26	27	28	29	30	31

JANUARY

FRIDAY
9

SATURDAY
10

SUNDAY
11

At Captain Parker's Warehouse in Merchant Taylors Hall in Threadneedle Street, near the Royal Exchange, are exposed for Sale, a Parcel of Turkey carpets, just arrived by the Fleet from Turkey, Twelve fine . . . carpets proper for Ladies Chambers or Dressing Rooms, and ninety two Pile Carpets, some fit to cover Drawing Rooms and Chambers, others of a smaller Size to put under Beds and Tables, in Dining-Rooms and Parlours, or by the Chimneys to sit on.

The Daily Courant of 27 November 1711.

January

WEEK 3

MONDAY ○
12

TUESDAY
13

WEDNESDAY
14

THURSDAY HOLIDAY, JAPAN
15

T	F	S	S	M	T	W	T	F	S	S	M	T	W	T	F	S	S	M	T	W	T	F	S	S	M	T	W	T	F	S
1	2	3	4	5	6	7	8	9	10	11	12	13	14	15	16	17	18	19	20	21	22	23	24	25	26	27	28	29	30	31

January

FRIDAY
16

SATURDAY
17

SUNDAY
18

Detail from a hand-knotted carpet designed by Ashley Havinden, probably for Edinburgh Weavers, Carlisle, about 1937.

T.380-1976

January

WEEK 4

MONDAY   Holiday, USA
19

TUESDAY
20

WEDNESDAY
21

THURSDAY
22

T	F	S	S	M	T	W	T	F	S	S	M	T	W	T	F	S	S	M	T	W	T	F	S	S	M	T	W	T	F	S
1	2	3	4	5	6	7	8	9	10	11	12	13	14	15	16	17	18	19	20	21	22	23	24	25	26	27	28	29	30	31

JANUARY

FRIDAY
23

SATURDAY
24

SUNDAY
25

The Ardabil Carpet was acquired by the South Kensington Museum in 1893 for £2,000. The previous highest price paid by the Museum had been £150 in 1890 for another 16th-century Persian carpet known as the Chelsea Carpet.

Overleaf: Detail from the Ardabil Carpet, one of the most famous Persian carpets, which is dated 946 in the Islamic calendar (1539–40 AD). It is named after a shrine in north-west Iran from where it is said to have come.

272-1893

January – February

WEEK 5

MONDAY
26

Holiday, Australia

TUESDAY
27

WEDNESDAY
28

● Three day holiday begins, China

THURSDAY
29

S	M	T	W	T	F	S	S	M	T	W	T	F	S		S	M	T	W	T	F	S	S	M	T	W	T	F	S
18	19	20	21	22	23	24	25	26	27	28	29	30	31		1	2	3	4	5	6	7	8	9	10	11	12	13	14

January – February

FRIDAY
30

SATURDAY
31

SUNDAY
1

In the 1890s one carpet workshop in Tabriz, owned by a Russian, employed up to 1,500 workers and had 100 carpets in production at any one time:
'Very expensive woollen and silk carpets were made, mostly based on European designs. The products were mostly exported to America and England.'

Translated from *Otchet o poezdke po Severnomu Azerbaidzhanu* by P. I. Averyanov, Tiflis, 1900.

February

WEEK 6

MONDAY
2

TUESDAY
3

WEDNESDAY
4

THURSDAY
5

S	M	T	W	T	F	S	S	M	T	W	T	F	S	S	M	T	W	T	F	S	S	M	T	W	T	F	S
1	2	3	4	5	6	7	8	9	10	11	12	13	14	15	16	17	18	19	20	21	22	23	24	25	26	27	28

February

Holiday, New Zealand

FRIDAY
6

SATURDAY
7

SUNDAY
8

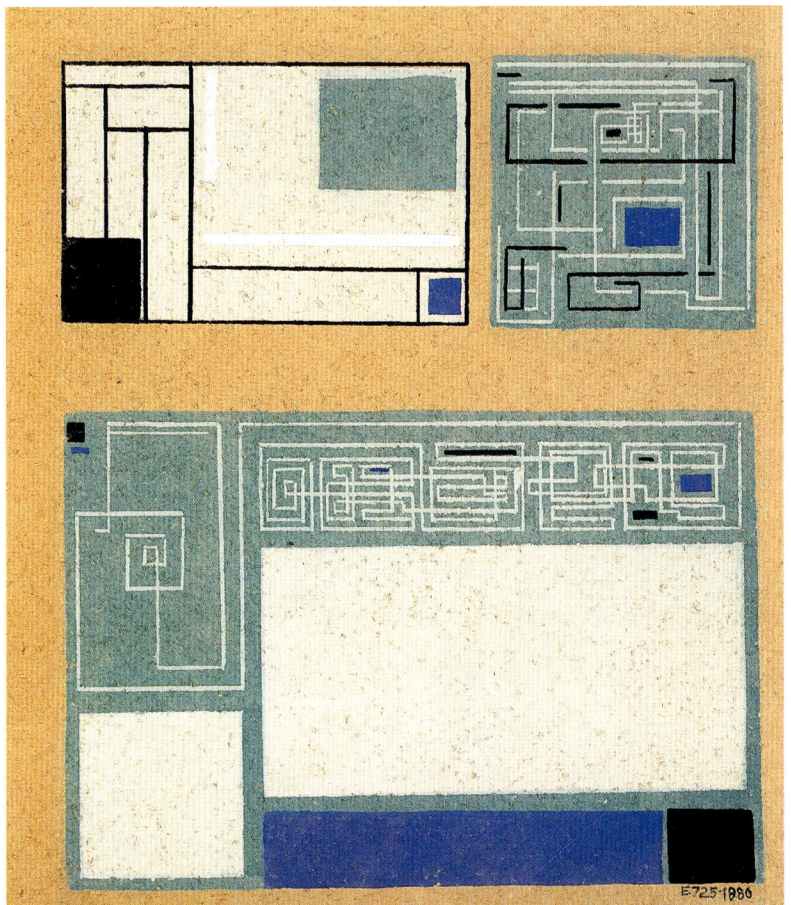

Design for a carpet by Francis Jourdain, from
Tapis Modernes, Paris 1930. Plate 21.
E725-1980

February

WEEK 7

MONDAY
9

TUESDAY
10

WEDNESDAY
11   ○ Holiday, China & Japan

THURSDAY
12

S	M	T	W	T	F	S	S	M	T	W	T	F	S	S	M	T	W	T	F	S	S	M	T	W	T	F	S
1	2	3	4	5	6	7	8	9	10	11	12	13	14	15	16	17	18	19	20	21	22	23	24	25	26	27	28

February

FRIDAY
13

SATURDAY
14

SUNDAY
15

T he upper-class householder in England and North America is rare who does not think the acquisition of such an article, whether genuine or spurious, an indispensable testimony both to culture and civilisation.

George Curzon, *Persia and the Persian Question*, 1892.

FEBRUARY

WEEK 8

MONDAY

HOLIDAY, USA

16

TUESDAY

17

WEDNESDAY

18

THURSDAY

19

S	M	T	W	T	F	S	S	M	T	W	T	F	S	S	M	T	W	T	F	S	S	M	T	W	T	F	S
1	2	3	4	5	6	7	8	9	10	11	12	13	14	15	16	17	18	19	20	21	22	23	24	25	26	27	28

February

FRIDAY
20

SATURDAY
21

SUNDAY
22

Part of a Spanish, 16th century knotted-pile hanging.
An area of old restoration can be seen slightly
above the middle.

841-1894

February – March

WEEK 9

MONDAY
23

TUESDAY
24
SHROVE TUESDAY

WEDNESDAY
25
ASH WEDNESDAY

THURSDAY
26
●

S M T W T F S S M T W T F S   S M T W T F S S M T W T F S
15 16 17 18 19 20 21 22 23 24 25 26 27 28   1 2 3 4 5 6 7 8 9 10 11 12 13 14

February – March

FRIDAY
27

SATURDAY
28

St. David's Day   SUNDAY
1

The old [oriental] carpets are generally long and narrow in form, a fact which makes it somewhat difficult to adapt them to European requirements; however, for ecclesiastical purposes they are invaluable, having a very rich appearance on the pure white marble steps of a chancel.

Advertising leaflet for George P. Baker, London, late 19th century.

Overleaf: 'Wessex': a hand-knotted carpet designed by Edward McKnight Kauffer in 1929 for The Wilton Royal Carpet Factory Ltd near Salisbury.
T.440-1971

March

WEEK 10

MONDAY
2

TUESDAY
3

WEDNESDAY
4

THURSDAY
5

S	M	T	W	T	F	S	S	M	T	W	T	F	S	S	M	T	W	T	F	S	S	M	T	W	T	F	S	S	M	T
1	2	3	4	5	6	7	8	9	10	11	12	13	14	15	16	17	18	19	20	21	22	23	24	25	26	27	28	29	30	31

March

FRIDAY
6

SATURDAY
7

HOLIDAY, CHINA

SUNDAY
8

A new Turcoman carpet is not a pleasing object to the European eye, its bright magentas and hard whites making a crude combination that gives little idea of the wonderful reds and creams that it will change into with the course of years...

Ella C Sykes, *Persia and its People*, London, 1910.

March

WEEK 11

MONDAY
9

COMMONWEALTH DAY

TUESDAY
10

WEDNESDAY
11

THURSDAY
12

MARCH

FRIDAY
13

SATURDAY
14

SUNDAY
15

Design for a rug by Kate Greenaway RI (1846–1901), from a set of six of conventional floral ornaments for textiles.
D1800-1904

March

WEEK 12

MONDAY
16

TUESDAY
17   HOLIDAY, NORTHERN IRELAND

WEDNESDAY
18

THURSDAY
19

S	M	T	W	T	F	S	S	M	T	W	T	F	S	S	M	T	W	T	F	S	S	M	T	W	T	F	S	S	M	T
1	2	3	4	5	6	7	8	9	10	11	12	13	14	15	16	17	18	19	20	21	22	23	24	25	26	27	28	29	30	31

March

Vernal Equinox, Spring begins   Holiday, Japan

FRIDAY

20

◐

SATURDAY

21

Mothering Sunday

SUNDAY

22

Bright colours could pose problems: G. P. Baker reported to his father that one batch of carpets received from Turkey was woven with colours which were 'very violent', making them 'only useful for the Americans'.

Letter Book, 19 January 1887.

March

WEEK 13

MONDAY
23

TUESDAY
24

WEDNESDAY
25

THURSDAY
26

S	M	T	W	T	F	S	S	M	T	W	T	F	S	S	M	T	W	T	F	S	S	M	T	W	T	F	S	S	M	T
1	2	3	4	5	6	7	8	9	10	11	12	13	14	15	16	17	18	19	20	21	22	23	24	25	26	27	28	29	30	31

MARCH

FRIDAY
27

SATURDAY
28

BRITISH SUMMER TIME BEGINS, UK

SUNDAY
29

'Daffodil and Bluebell': a sample of machine-woven Brussels
carpeting designed by Walter Crane in 1896 for
J. Templeton & Co., Glasgow.

T.99-1953

March – April

WEEK 14

MONDAY
30

TUESDAY
31

WEDNESDAY
1

THURSDAY
2

March – April

FRIDAY
3

SATURDAY
4

Palm Sunday   Holiday, China
DST begins, USA

SUNDAY
5

The female members of the family are mainly occupied in household duties. They do all the cooking and fetching water, and the daughters for whom there is no other occupation occupy themselves in the manufacture of embroidered skull-caps, carpets, shirts, saddle-bags, and socks of variegated tints.

Edmund O'Donovan, *The Merv Oasis*, London, 1882.

Overleaf: A detail from the border of the Bradford Table Carpet, linen embroidered with silk in tent stitch. It was probably made in London and dates from the early 17th century.

T.134-1928

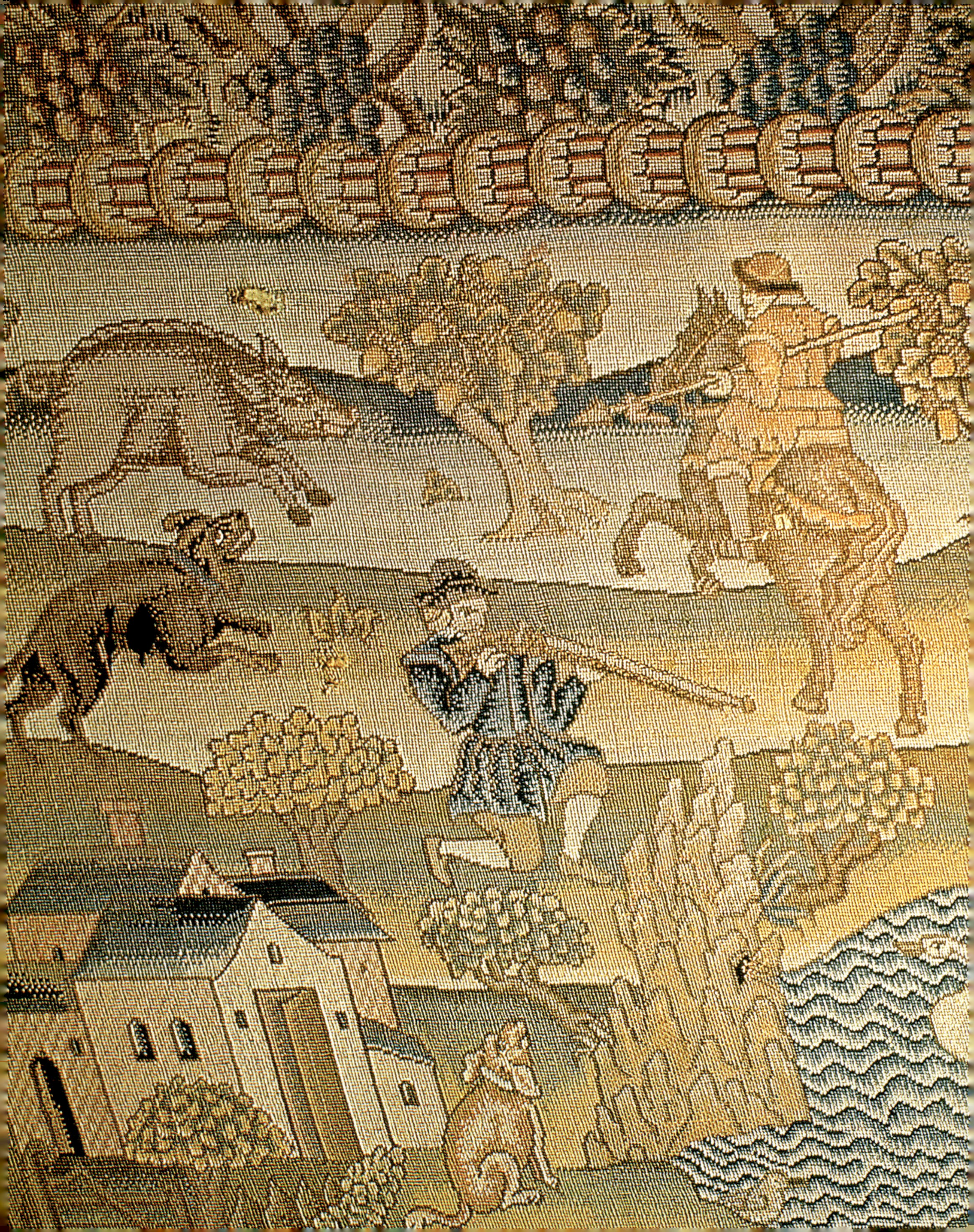

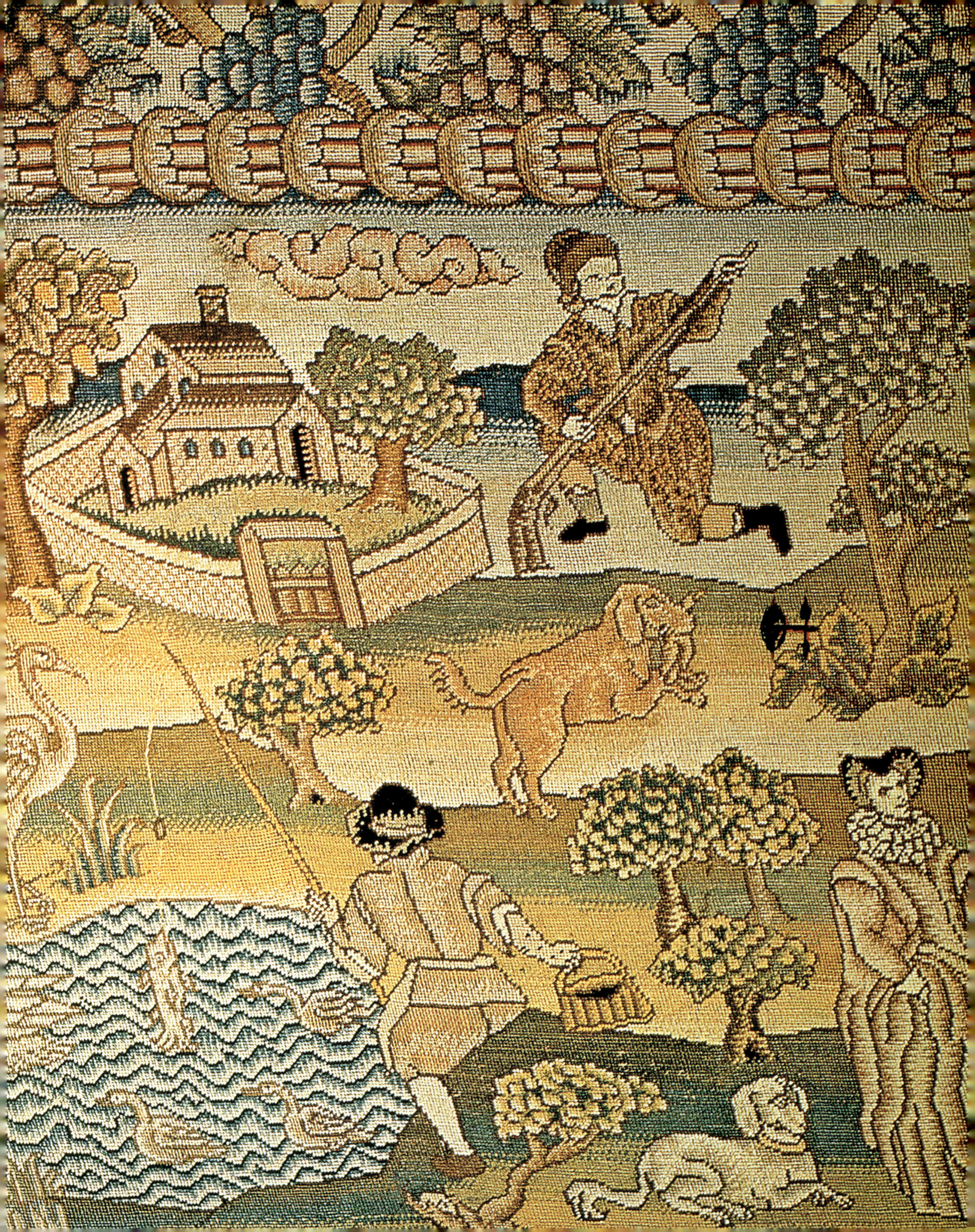

April

WEEK 15

Monday
6

Tuesday
7

Wednesday
8

Thursday
9

W T F S S M T W T F S S M T W T F S S M T W T F S S M T W T
1 2 3 4 5 6 7 8 9 10 11 12 13 14 15 16 17 18 19 20 21 22 23 24 25 26 27 28 29 30

April

GOOD FRIDAY   HOLIDAY, UK, AUSTRALIA, CANADA, NEW ZEALAND & GERMANY

FRIDAY
10

○ FIRST DAY OF PASSOVER (PESACH)   HOLIDAY, AUSTRALIA

SATURDAY
11

EASTER SUNDAY

SUNDAY
12

Until the 1880s the bulk of carpet weaving was done in the weaver's home, with the manufacturer providing the design and the dyed wool. In Tabriz, 'The practice has the usual disadvantages of home employment, slovenly and dilatory work, with little progress towards skill and finish, as the looms, scattered over a wide area, cannot be constantly inspected.'

'Report on the Trade of Tabriz in 1877', *Correspondance Commerciale, 1897*, Ministère des Affaires Etrangères, France.

April

WEEK 16

MONDAY
13
HOLIDAY, UK EXC SCOTLAND, FRANCE, ITALY, GERMANY, AUSTRALIA, NEW ZEALAND & CANADA

TUESDAY
14

WEDNESDAY
15

THURSDAY
16

W T F S S M T W T F S S M T W T F S S M T W T F S S M T W T
1 2 3 4 5 6 7 8 9 10 11 12 13 14 15 16 17 18 19 20 21 22 23 24 25 26 27 28 29 30

APRIL

FRIDAY
17

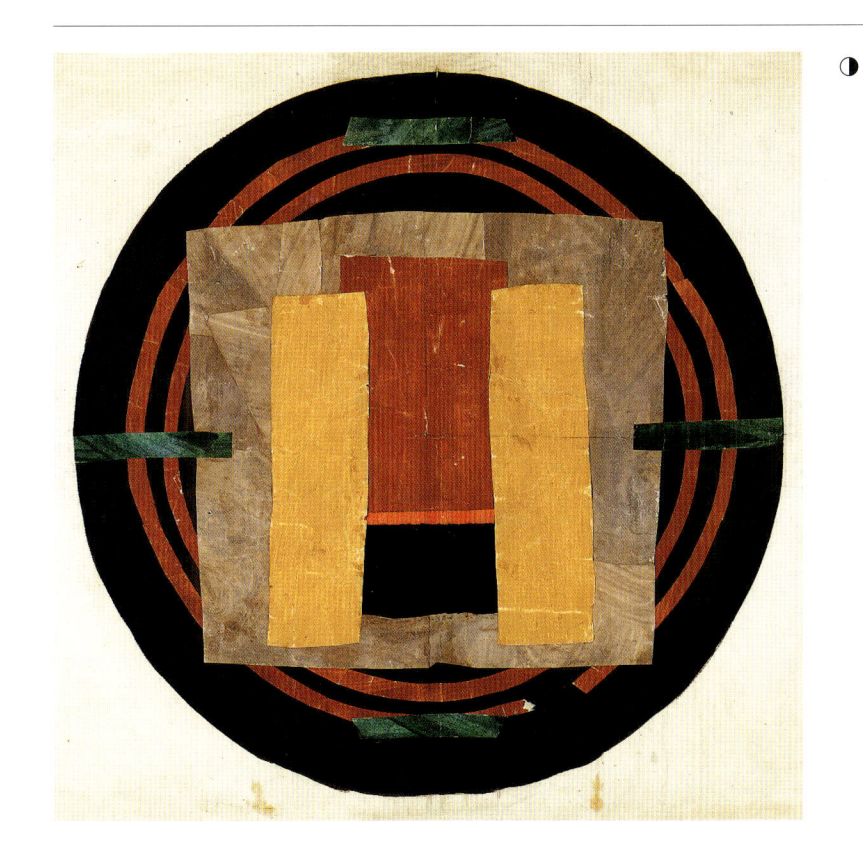

SATURDAY
18

SUNDAY
19

Design for a rug by Vanessa Bell. Omega Workshops, London.
E722-1955

APRIL

WEEK 17

MONDAY
20

TUESDAY
21
BIRTHDAY OF QUEEN ELIZABETH II

WEDNESDAY
22

THURSDAY
23
ST. GEORGE'S DAY

APRIL

HOLIDAY, ITALY

FRIDAY
24

SATURDAY
25

● **SUNDAY**
26

Each girl usually manufactures two extra fine carpets, to form part of her dowry when she marries. When this has been done, she devotes herself to producing goods for the markets at Meshed and Bokhara.

Edmund O'Donovan, *The Merv Oasis*, London, 1882.

Overleaf: This is the decorative knotted-pile panel (called a bag face) from the front of a storage bag and was woven by the Salor nomads of western central Asia in the middle of the 19th century.

2324-1876

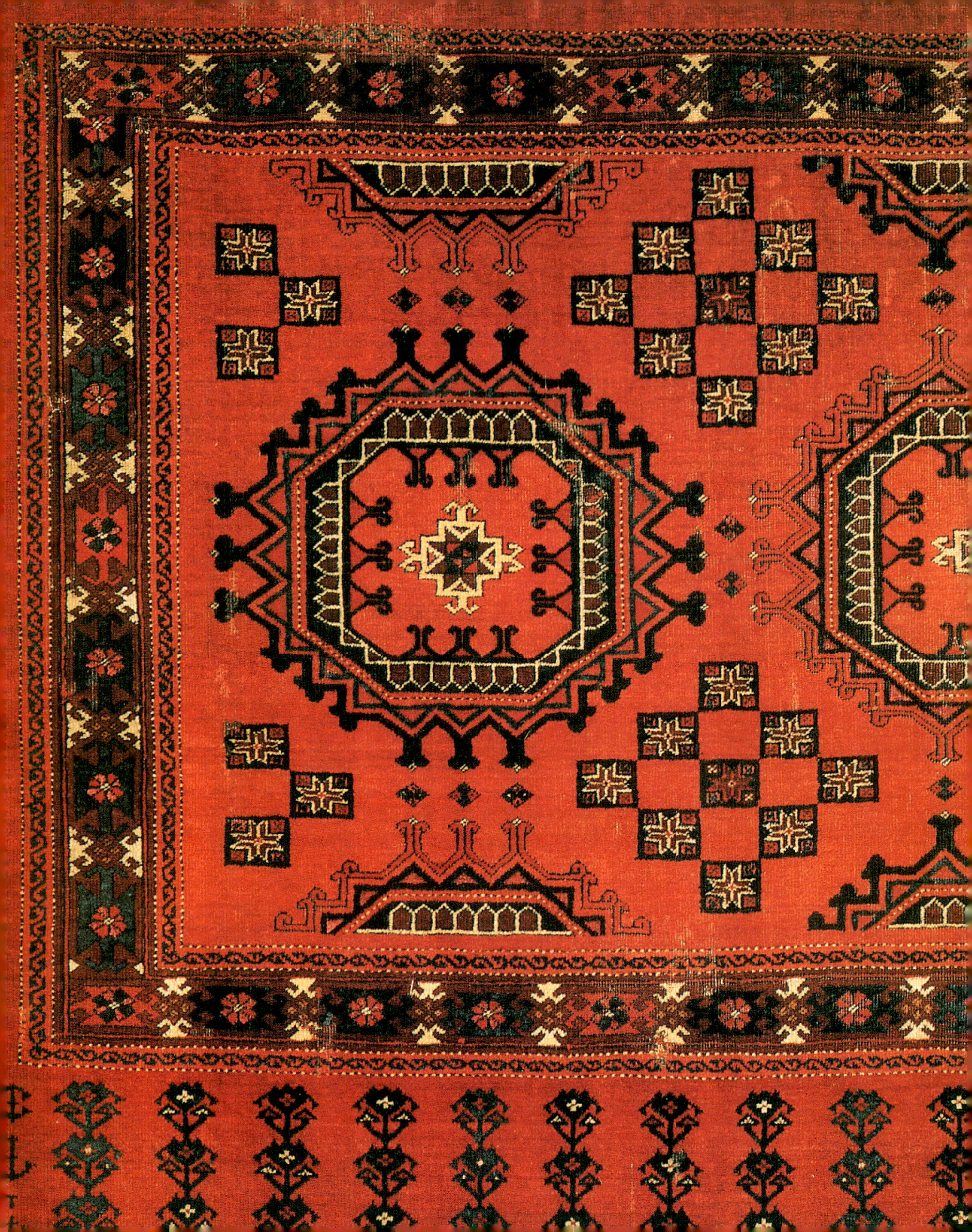

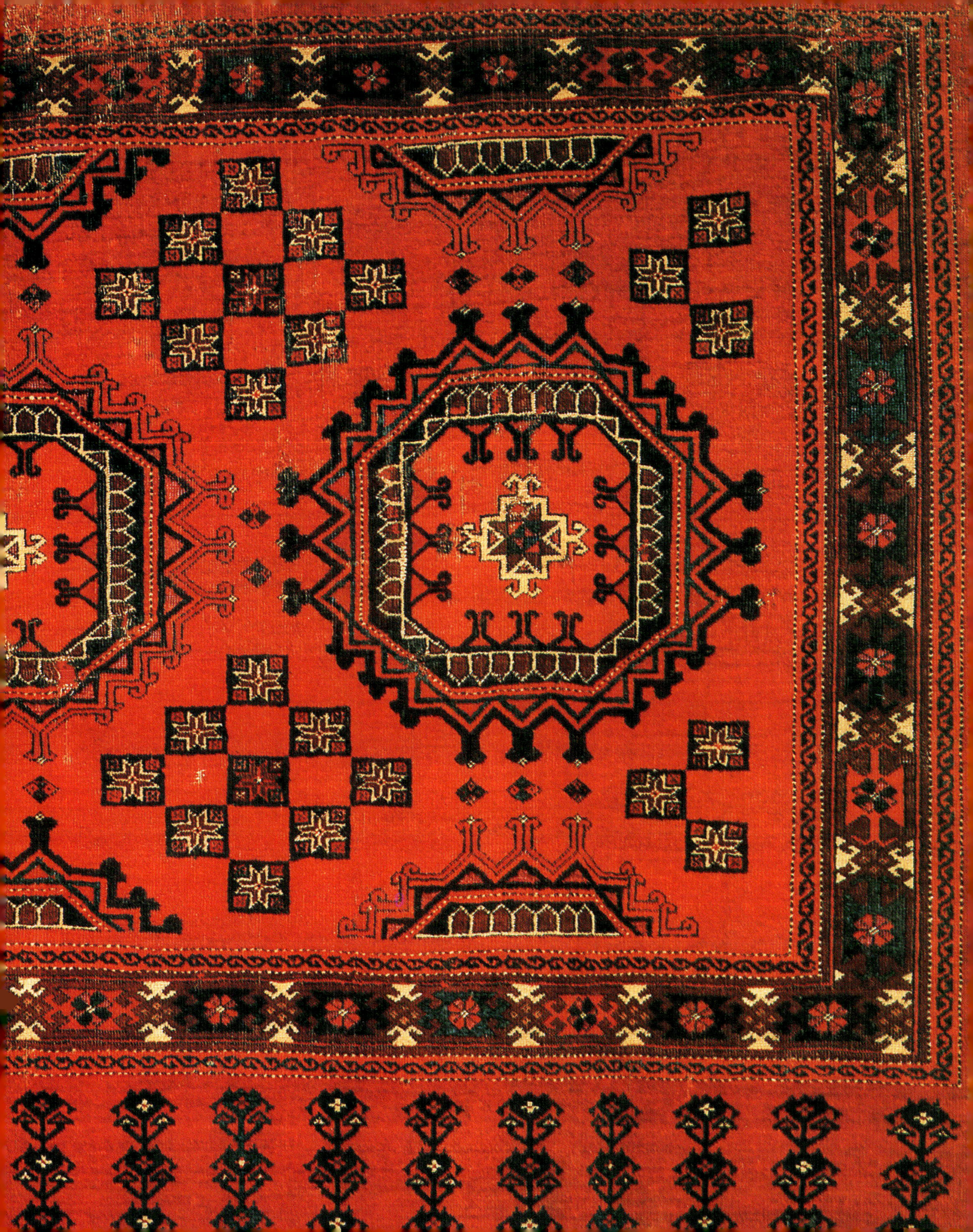

April – May

WEEK 18

MONDAY   Holiday, Australia
27

TUESDAY   Islamic New Year begins
28

WEDNESDAY   Holiday, Japan
29

THURSDAY
30

F	S	S	M	T	W	T	F	S	S	M	T	W	T		F	S	S	M	T	W	T	F	S	S	M	T	W	T
17	18	19	20	21	22	23	24	25	26	27	28	29	30		1	2	3	4	5	6	7	8	9	10	11	12	13	14

April – May

Holiday, France, Germany, Italy & China

FRIDAY
1

SATURDAY
2

◐ Holiday, Japan

SUNDAY
3

The beautiful carpets made in the town will attract him; but if he visits a factory and observes that the children who make the artistic fabrics are crippled and deformed from the long hours of work, and diseased from the dark, damp places in which they are forced to spend their days of labour, he will feel that the price of a Kerman carpet is a heavy one.

Ella C. Sykes *Persia and its People*, London, 1910.

May

WEEK 19

Monday
4

Holiday, UK (TBC)

Tuesday
5

Holiday, Japan

Wednesday
6

Thursday
7

F	S	S	M	T	W	T	F	S	S	M	T	W	T	F	S	S	M	T	W	T	F	S	S	M	T	W	T	F	S	S
1	2	3	4	5	6	7	8	9	10	11	12	13	14	15	16	17	18	19	20	21	22	23	24	25	26	27	28	29	30	31

MAY

HOLIDAY, FRANCE

FRIDAY
8

SATURDAY
9

SUNDAY
10

Design for a carpet by Gunda Stolzl.
German, 1928 Bauhaus.
CIRC 697-1967

MAY

WEEK 20

MONDAY ○
11

TUESDAY
12

WEDNESDAY
13

THURSDAY
14

| F | S | S | M | T | W | T | F | S | S | M | T | W | T | F | S | S | M | T | W | T | F | S | S | M | T | W | T | F | S | S |
| 1 | 2 | 3 | 4 | 5 | 6 | 7 | 8 | 9 | 10 | 11 | 12 | 13 | 14 | 15 | 16 | 17 | 18 | 19 | 20 | 21 | 22 | 23 | 24 | 25 | 26 | 27 | 28 | 29 | 30 | 31 |

May

Friday
15

Saturday
16

Sunday
17

At the beginning of the 20th century the acting British Consul in Kerman, Major Phillott, 'was so horrified at what he saw of the state of these little sufferers, that he determined to start a loom of his own, employing men only to do the weaving. This he accordingly did, finding, of course, that the expense was enormous, as men's wages were so much higher than the children's, and also that they would not consent to such long hours.'

M. E. Hume-Griffith, *Behind the Veil in Persia and Turkish Arabia*, London, 1909.

May

WEEK 21

MONDAY
18

HOLIDAY, CANADA

TUESDAY
19

WEDNESDAY
20

THURSDAY
21

HOLIDAY, FRANCE & GERMANY

F	S	S	M	T	W	T	F	S	S	M	T	W	T	F	S	S	M	T	W	T	F	S	S	M	T	W	T	F	S	S
1	2	3	4	5	6	7	8	9	10	11	12	13	14	15	16	17	18	19	20	21	22	23	24	25	26	27	28	29	30	31

May

FRIDAY
22

SATURDAY
23

SUNDAY
24

Part of 'Carbrook', a hand-knotted carpet designed by
William Morris and woven for 1 Holland Park in 1883.
CIRC.458-1965

May

WEEK 22

MONDAY
25

● Holiday, UK & USA

TUESDAY
26

WEDNESDAY
27

THURSDAY
28

F	S	S	M	T	W	T	F	S	S	M	T	W	T	F	S	S	M	T	W	T	F	S	S	M	T	W	T	F	S	S
1	2	3	4	5	6	7	8	9	10	11	12	13	14	15	16	17	18	19	20	21	22	23	24	25	26	27	28	29	30	31

MAY

FRIDAY
29

Holiday, China

SATURDAY
30

Feast of Weeks (Shavuot)
Whit Sunday

SUNDAY
31

In that town [Kerman] opium-smoking parents make contracts for their children with master carpet weavers, taking money in advance if they can. So little girls of five, six or seven are bound for periods of one or two years, working daily from soon after sunrise till about sunset, in dark, ill-ventilated, dirty, mud hovels, at the hand carpet looms.

Clara C. Rice, *Mary Bird in Persia*, London, 1916.

Overleaf: Detail from the Salting Carpet which is the centre of current controversy: some think it is 16th-century Persian while others think it is mid-19th-century Turkish. The design is certainly Persian in character but the brightness of the colours suggests a late date.
T.404-1910

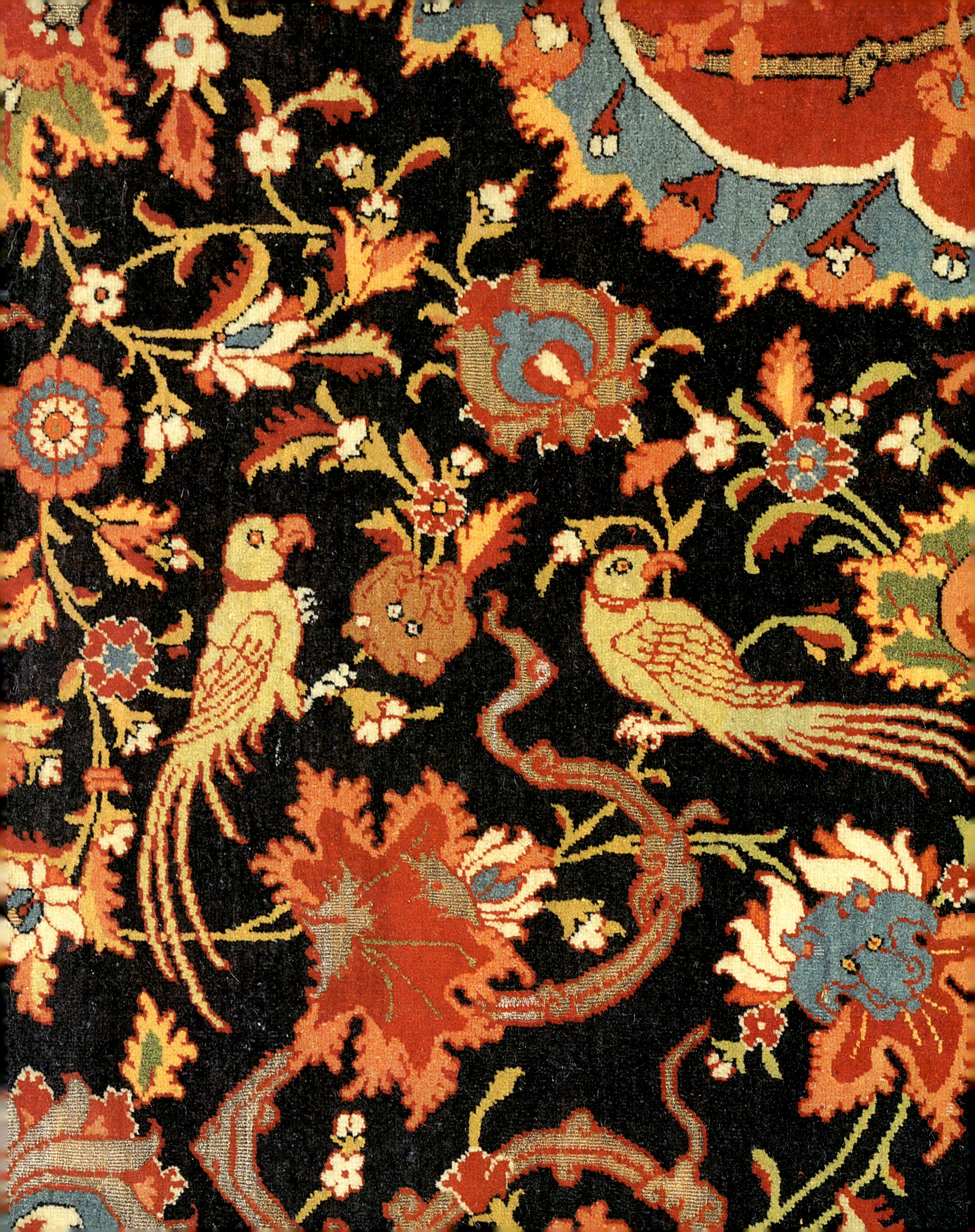

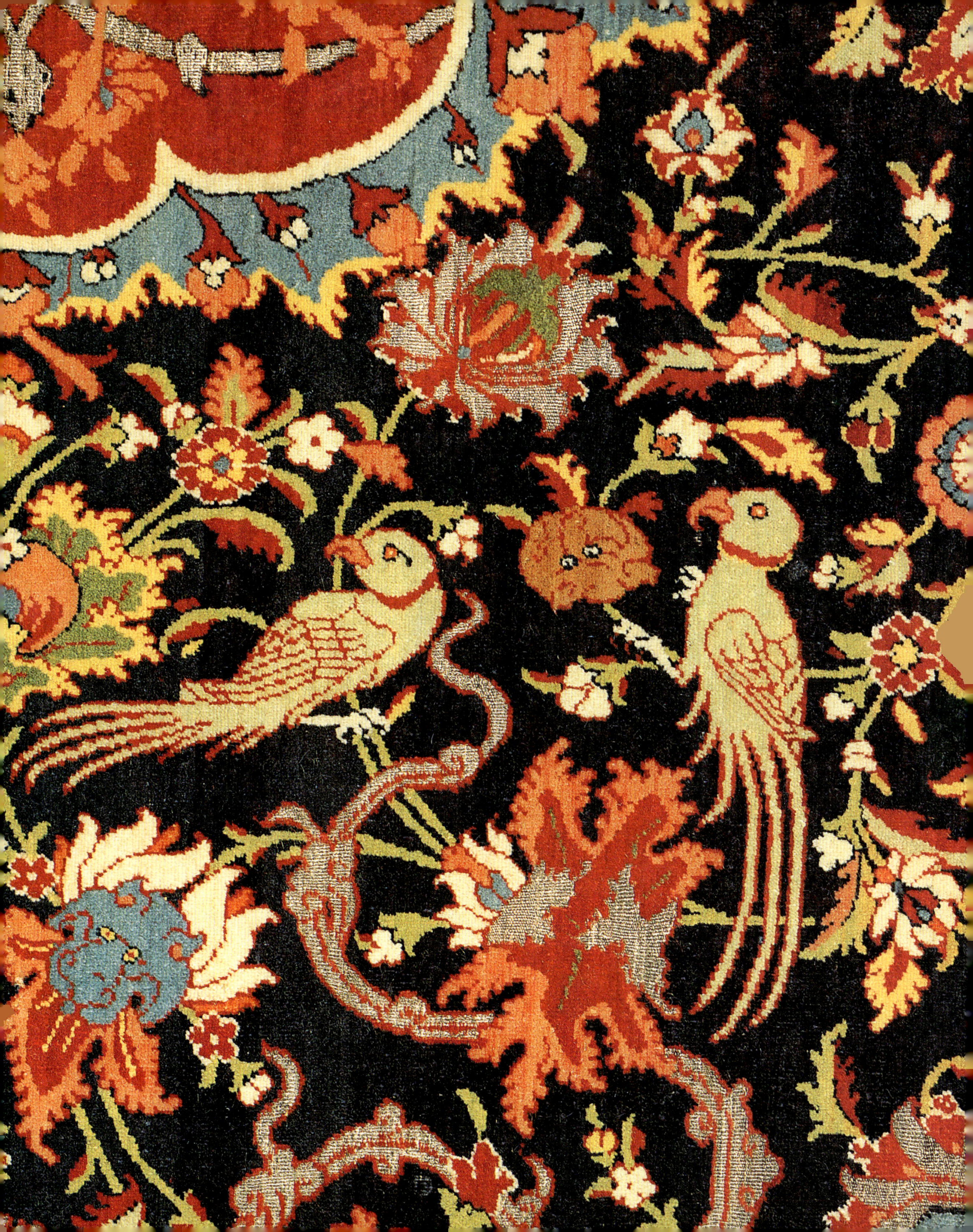

June

WEEK 23

MONDAY   Holiday, New Zealand, France & Germany
1

TUESDAY ◐
2

WEDNESDAY
3

THURSDAY
4

M	T	W	T	F	S	S	M	T	W	T	F	S	S	M	T	W	T	F	S	S	M	T	W	T	F	S	S	M	T
1	2	3	4	5	6	7	8	9	10	11	12	13	14	15	16	17	18	19	20	21	22	23	24	25	26	27	28	29	30

June

Holiday, China

FRIDAY
5

SATURDAY
6

SUNDAY
7

In some places, particularly at Kerman, the manufacture is pursued under very unhealthy conditions, the artisans being obliged to work underground in order to escape the dryness of the outer air, while the elasticity of the threads is preserved by moisture from vessels filled with water.

George N. Curzon, *Persia and the Persian Question*, London. 1892.

June

WEEK 24

MONDAY
8

TUESDAY
9

WEDNESDAY
10
○ Birthday of Prince Philip, Duke of Edinburgh

THURSDAY
11

M	T	W	T	F	S	S	M	T	W	T	F	S	S	M	T	W	T	F	S	S	M	T	W	T	F	S	S	M	T
1	2	3	4	5	6	7	8	9	10	11	12	13	14	15	16	17	18	19	20	21	22	23	24	25	26	27	28	29	30

June

FRIDAY
12

The Queen's Official Birthday (TBC)

SATURDAY
13

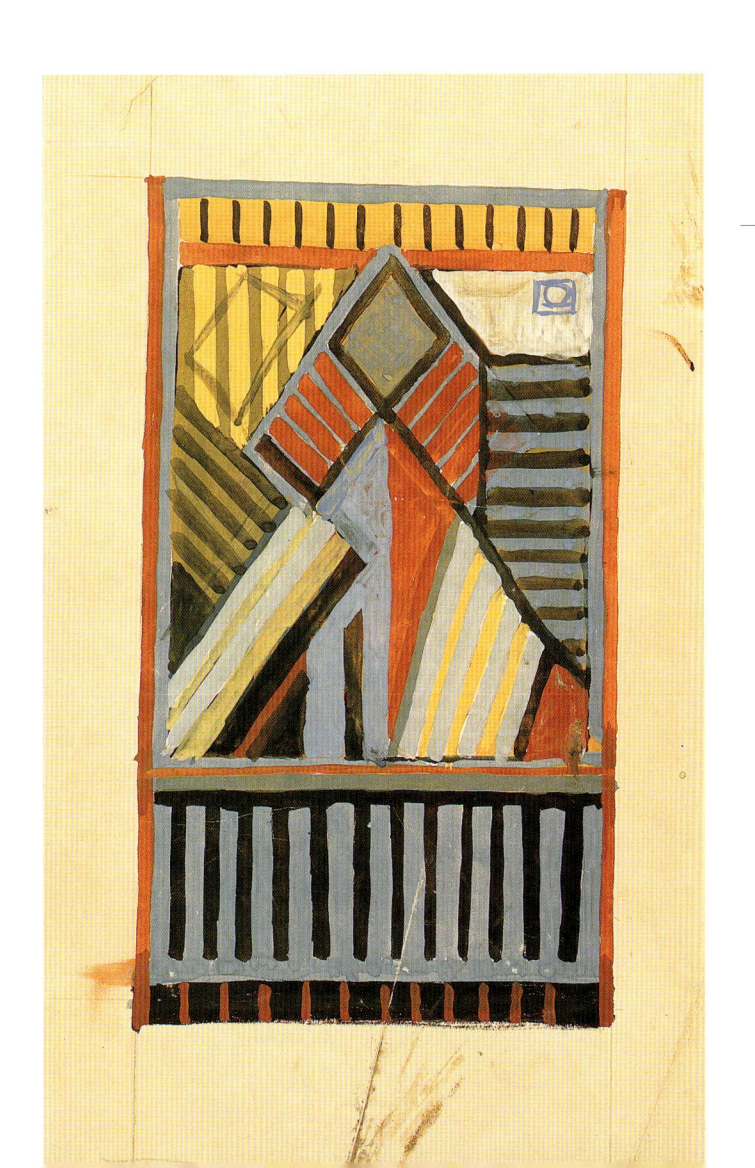

SUNDAY
14

Design by Fred Etchells for Ideal Home Exhibition rug.
Watercolour. Omega Workshops, London.

E730-1955

JUNE

WEEK 25

MONDAY
15

HOLIDAY, AUSTRALIA

TUESDAY
16

WEDNESDAY
17

◐

THURSDAY
18

June

FRIDAY
19

SATURDAY
20

Summer Solstice, Summer begins
Father's Day, UK

SUNDAY
21

William Morris 'deplored the decline in standards in imported contemporary eastern rugs at this time, due primarily to the use of artificial dyestuffs and the mass-production of indifferent, westernized designs to satisfy a large and enthusiastic export market'.

Linda Parry, *William Morris Textiles*, London, 1983.

June

WEEK 26

MONDAY
22

TUESDAY
23

WEDNESDAY
24   ●

THURSDAY
25

M T W T F S S M T W T F S S M T W T F S S M T W T F S S M T
1 2 3 4 5 6 7 8 9 10 11 12 13 14 15 16 17 18 19 20 21 22 23 24 25 26 27 28 29 30

June

FRIDAY
26

SATURDAY
27

SUNDAY
28

A Norwegian tapestry-woven cover from the late 18th or early 19th century.

T.13-1911

June – July

WEEK 27

MONDAY
29

TUESDAY
30

WEDNESDAY
1

◐ Holiday, Canada

THURSDAY
2

W T F S S M T W T F S S M T
17 18 19 20 21 22 23 24 25 26 27 28 29 30

W T F S S M T W T F S S M T
1 2 3 4 5 6 7 8 9 10 11 12 13 14

June – July

FRIDAY
3

Holiday, USA

SATURDAY
4

SUNDAY
5

In the 1850s Jakob Polak reported
that the carpet industry in Persia was in decline:
he could buy a carpet measuring 18′ × 9′
for between 12 and 40 ducats, yet a woollen
shawl would have cost at
least 50-60 ducats.

Persien, das Land und seine Bewohner, Leipzig, 1865.

Overleaf: Detail of the corner of a late 19th-century carpet
from the Kurdistan area of western Persia showing the
thick, richly coloured pile often associated with carpets
from this region.

258-1892

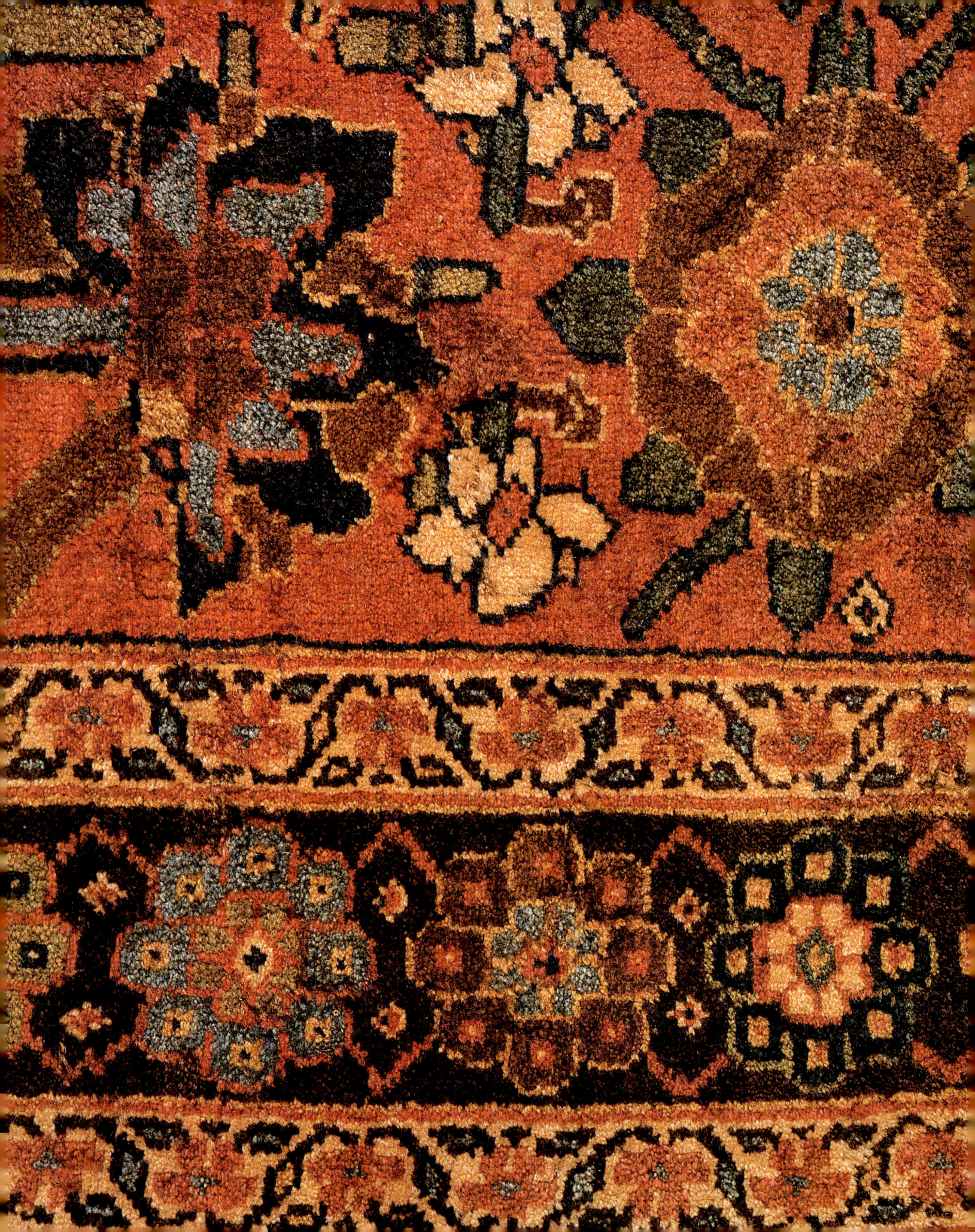

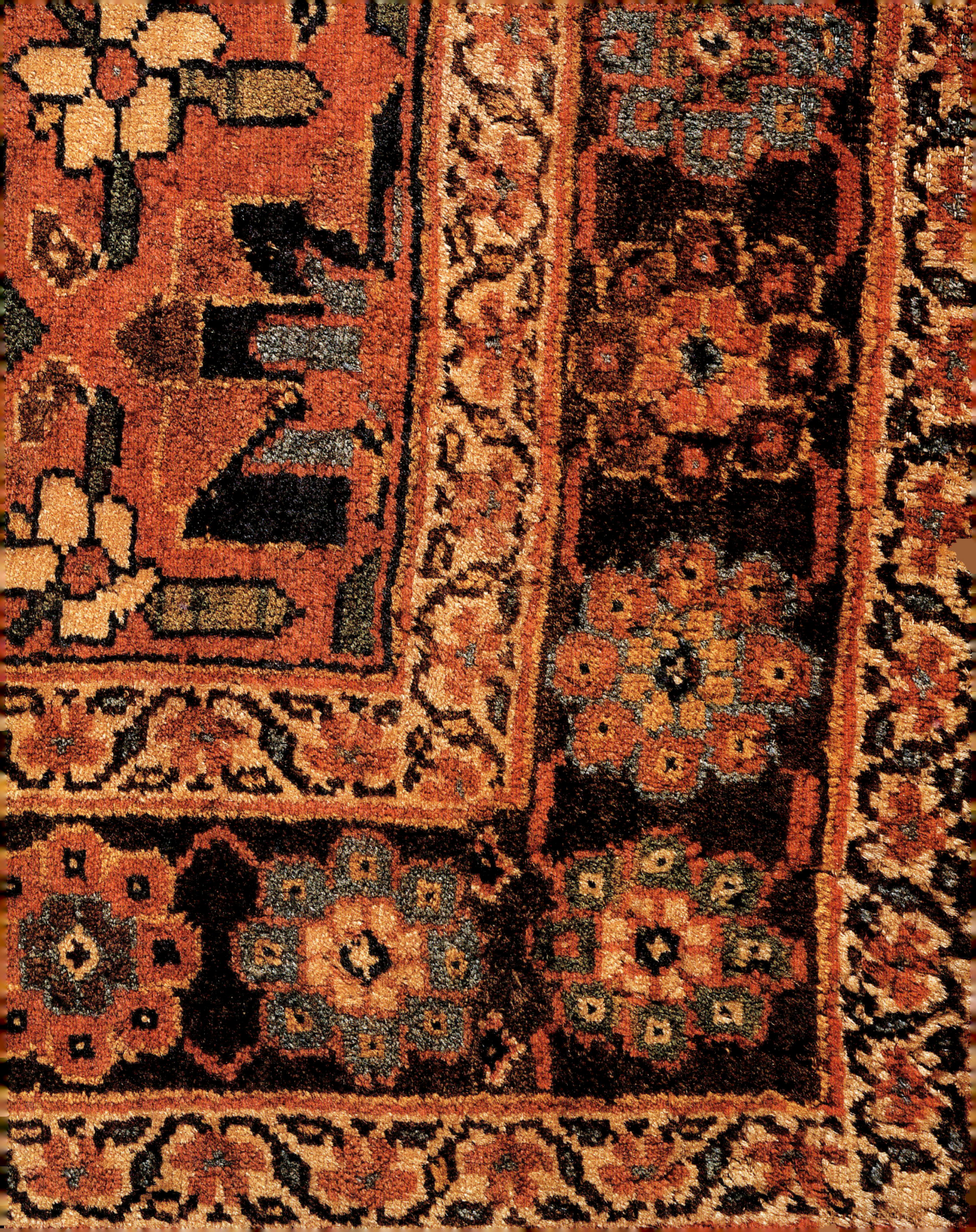

July

WEEK 28

MONDAY
6

TUESDAY
7

WEDNESDAY
8

THURSDAY
9 ○

W T F S S M T W T F S S M T W T F S S M T W T F S S M T W T F
1 2 3 4 5 6 7 8 9 10 11 12 13 14 15 16 17 18 19 20 21 22 23 24 25 26 27 28 29 30 31

July

FRIDAY
10

SATURDAY
11

SUNDAY
12

There have been several occasions on which very specific scientific examinations have helped to date carpets; one carpet from the Victoria & Albert Museum was bought in 1933 as a Turkish carpet dating from the late 17th century. In 1962 samples of the dyes were analyzed and the results indicated the presence of brilliant purpurine 10 B, invented in 1867, and a fusion of chrysophenine, which was invented in 1885. It now seems that the carpet was woven in eastern Europe, most likely in Romania, shortly before its purchase.

July

WEEK 29

MONDAY   Holiday, Northern Ireland (TBC)
13

TUESDAY   Holiday, France
14

WEDNESDAY
15

THURSDAY ◐
16

W	T	F	S	S	M	T	W	T	F	S	S	M	T	W	T	F	S	S	M	T	W	T	F	S	S	M	T	W	T	F
1	2	3	4	5	6	7	8	9	10	11	12	13	14	15	16	17	18	19	20	21	22	23	24	25	26	27	28	29	30	31

July

FRIDAY
17

SATURDAY
18

SUNDAY
19

Design for a carpet by Serge Gladky. Compositional decoratives, Plate 33. Nouvelles Compositions Décoratives (1re Série). Date Unknown.

E690-1980

July

WEEK 30

MONDAY
20
HOLIDAY, JAPAN

TUESDAY
21

WEDNESDAY
22

THURSDAY
23 ●

W	T	F	S	S	M	T	W	T	F	S	S	M	T	W	T	F	S	S	M	T	W	T	F	S	S	M	T	W	T	F
1	2	3	4	5	6	7	8	9	10	11	12	13	14	15	16	17	18	19	20	21	22	23	24	25	26	27	28	29	30	31

July

FRIDAY
24

SATURDAY
25

SUNDAY
26

The vegetable fibre, cotton, is normally used
in the pile only when a good-quality
white is needed, but it is probably the best fibre
for the warp and weft because it is not
very elastic and, unlike wool, it shrinks evenly;
a cotton foundation will produce
a firm, solid and heavy carpet.

Overleaf: A 15th-century carpet from southern Spain.
The basic design of octagons within rectangular panels was
copied from Turkish carpets of that time, but the fine
detail is a Spanish addition.

784-1905

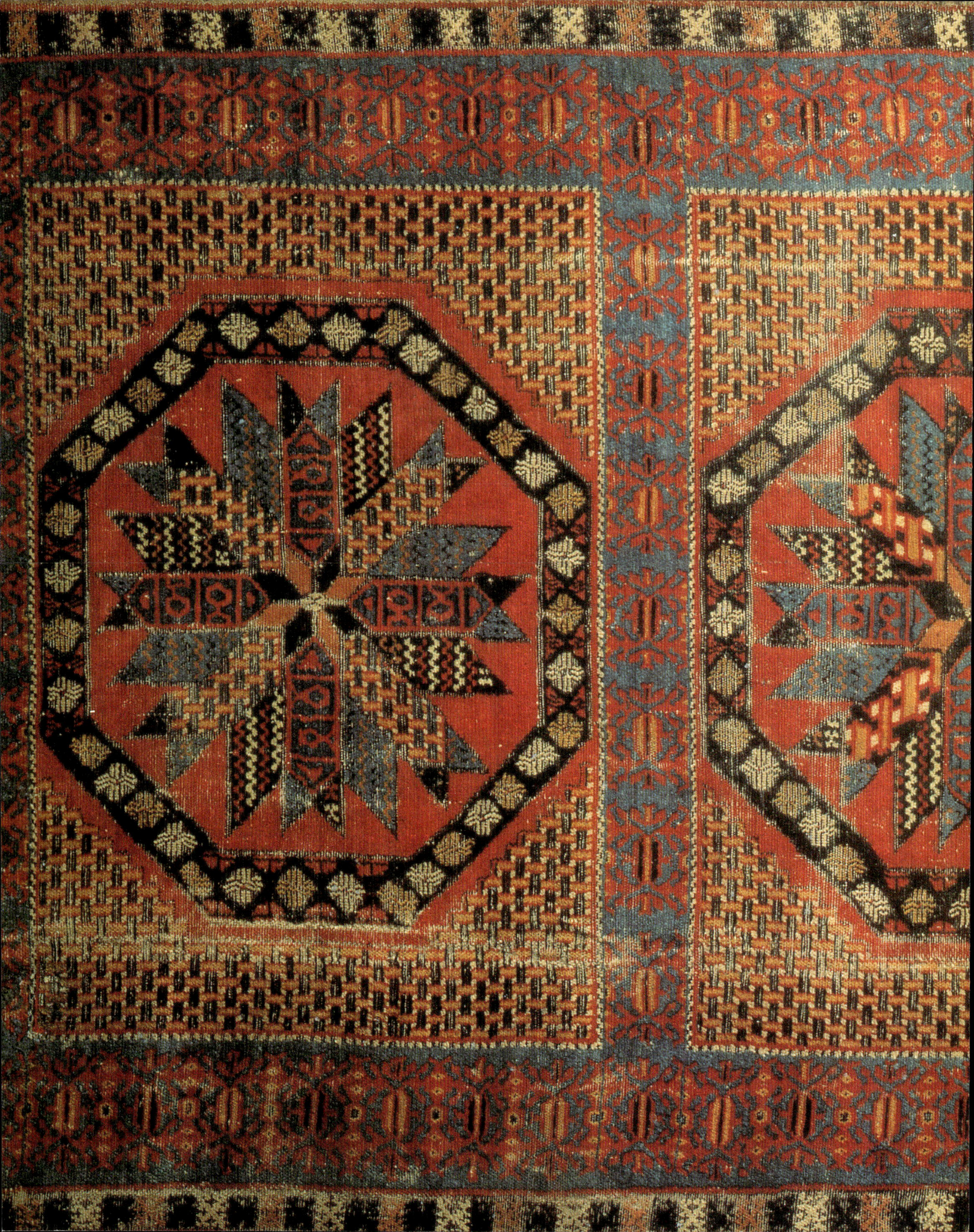

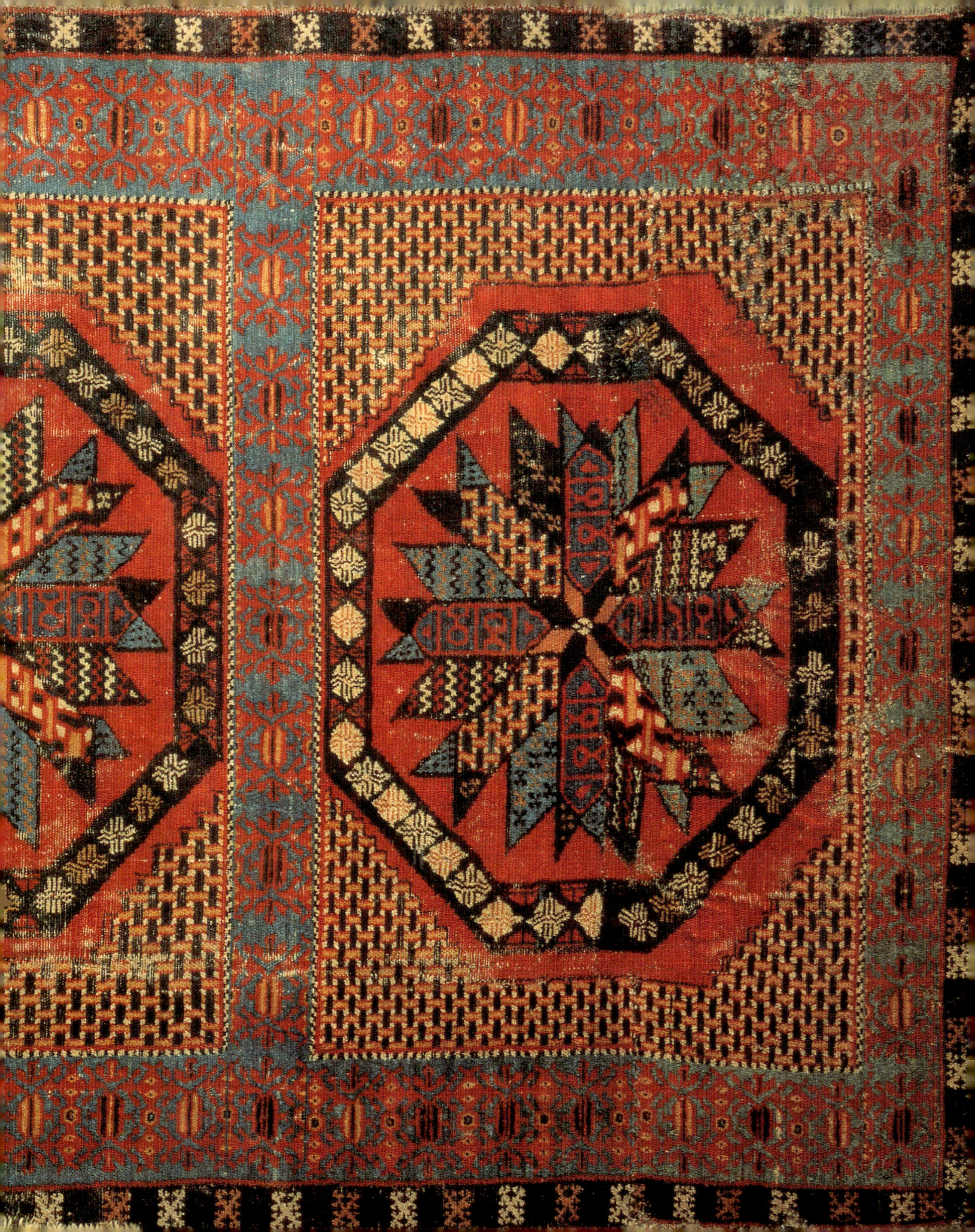

July – August

WEEK 31

MONDAY
27

TUESDAY
28

WEDNESDAY
29

THURSDAY
30

July – August

FRIDAY
31

SATURDAY
1

SUNDAY
2

Unlike those in the Sahara, camels in the colder climates of Persia and Afghanistan produce wool. Camel wool is usually found undyed in the pile, where it will add the required shades of brown. Goat hair is difficult to spin but is strong, and so it is sometimes used in the warp, for oversewing the sides of carpets and in added fringes and tassels.

AUGUST

WEEK 32

MONDAY
3

HOLIDAY, SCOTLAND

TUESDAY
4

WEDNESDAY
5

THURSDAY
6

S	M	T	W	T	F	S	S	M	T	W	T	F	S	S	M	T	W	T	F	S	S	M	T	W	T	F	S	S	M	T
1	2	3	4	5	6	7	8	9	10	11	12	13	14	15	16	17	18	19	20	21	22	23	24	25	26	27	28	29	30	31

AUGUST

FRIDAY
7

SATURDAY
8

○

SUNDAY
9

Design for a cadena rug by Roger Fry. Omega
Workshops, London, 1914.
E724-1955

August

WEEK 33

MONDAY
10

TUESDAY
11

WEDNESDAY
12

THURSDAY
13

S	M	T	W	T	F	S	S	M	T	W	T	F	S	S	M	T	W	T	F	S	S	M	T	W	T	F	S	S	M
1	2	3	4	5	6	7	8	9	10	11	12	13	14	15	16	17	18	19	20	21	22	23	24	25	26	27	28	29	30	31

AUGUST

FRIDAY
14

SATURDAY
15

Holiday, Italy

SUNDAY
16

Wool is strong, suitable for use as foundation thread and pile; it is available in abundance, readily accepts dyes and, although it can shrink unevenly and it stretches, it is the most important fibre used in carpets.

August

WEEK 34

MONDAY
17

TUESDAY
18

WEDNESDAY
19

THURSDAY
20

August

FRIDAY
21

SATURDAY
22

SUNDAY
23

Fragment of a 17th-century Caucasian carpet showing part of one border.
CIRC.376-1923

AUGUST

WEEK 35

MONDAY
24

TUESDAY
25

WEDNESDAY
26

THURSDAY
27

S	M	T	W	T	F	S	S	M	T	W	T	F	S	S	M	T	W	T	F	S	S	M	T	W	T	F	S	S	M
1	2	3	4	5	6	7	8	9	10	11	12	13	14	15	16	17	18	19	20	21	22	23	24	25	26	27	28	29	30	31

AUGUST

FRIDAY
28

SATURDAY
29

SUNDAY
30

Wool from upland-grazing sheep is better than wool from sheep grazing on lowland pastures. 'The Kerman carpets are extremely fine in texture, and it is said that the wool of which they are made owes its special quality to the herbage on which the sheep feed, and that if the animals are transported to other parts of Persia their fleeces would become coarser in fibre.

Ella C Sykes, *Persia and its People*, London, 1910.

Overleaf: Detail from a hand-knotted carpet which is probably French and dates from 1923–25.
T.393-1977

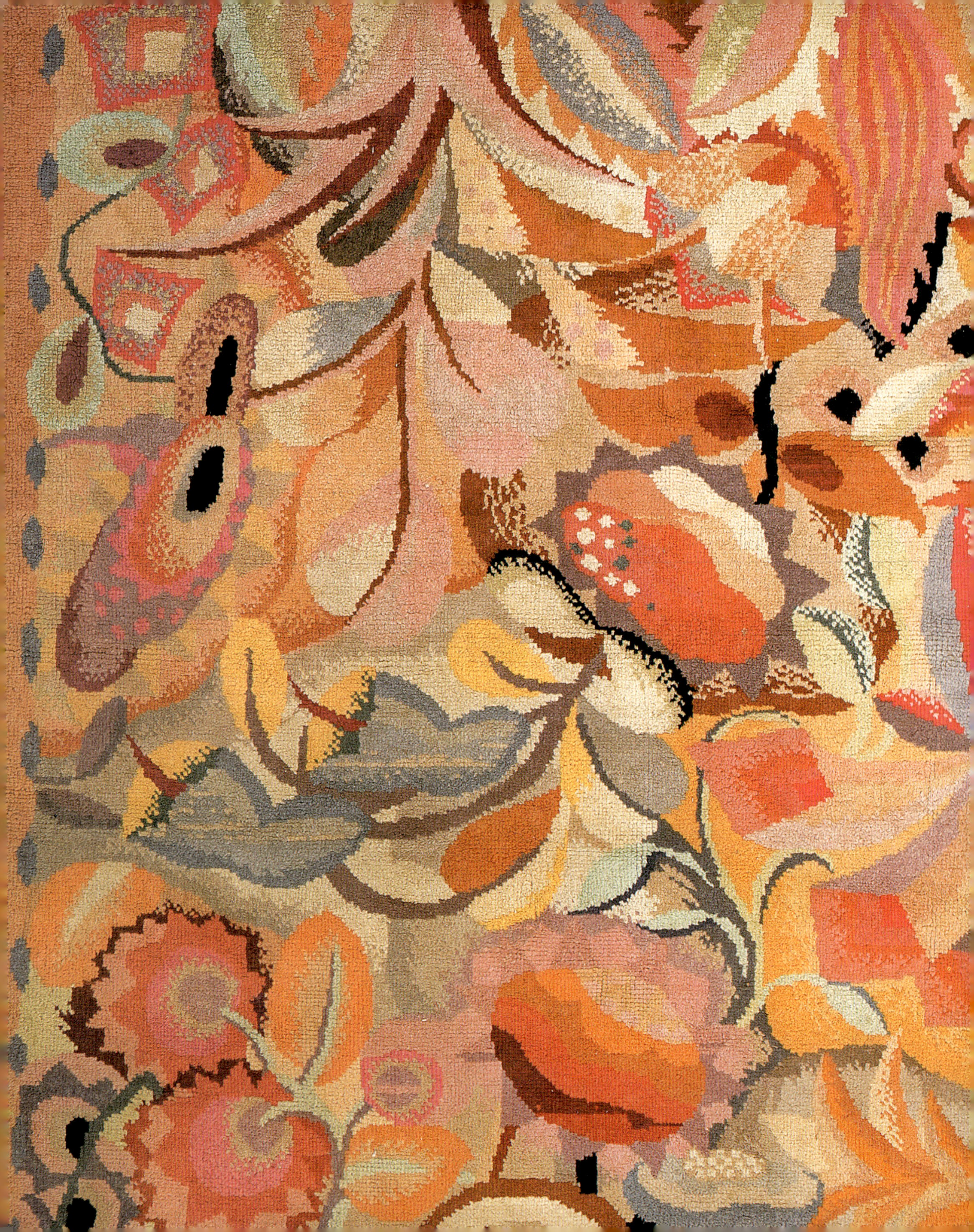

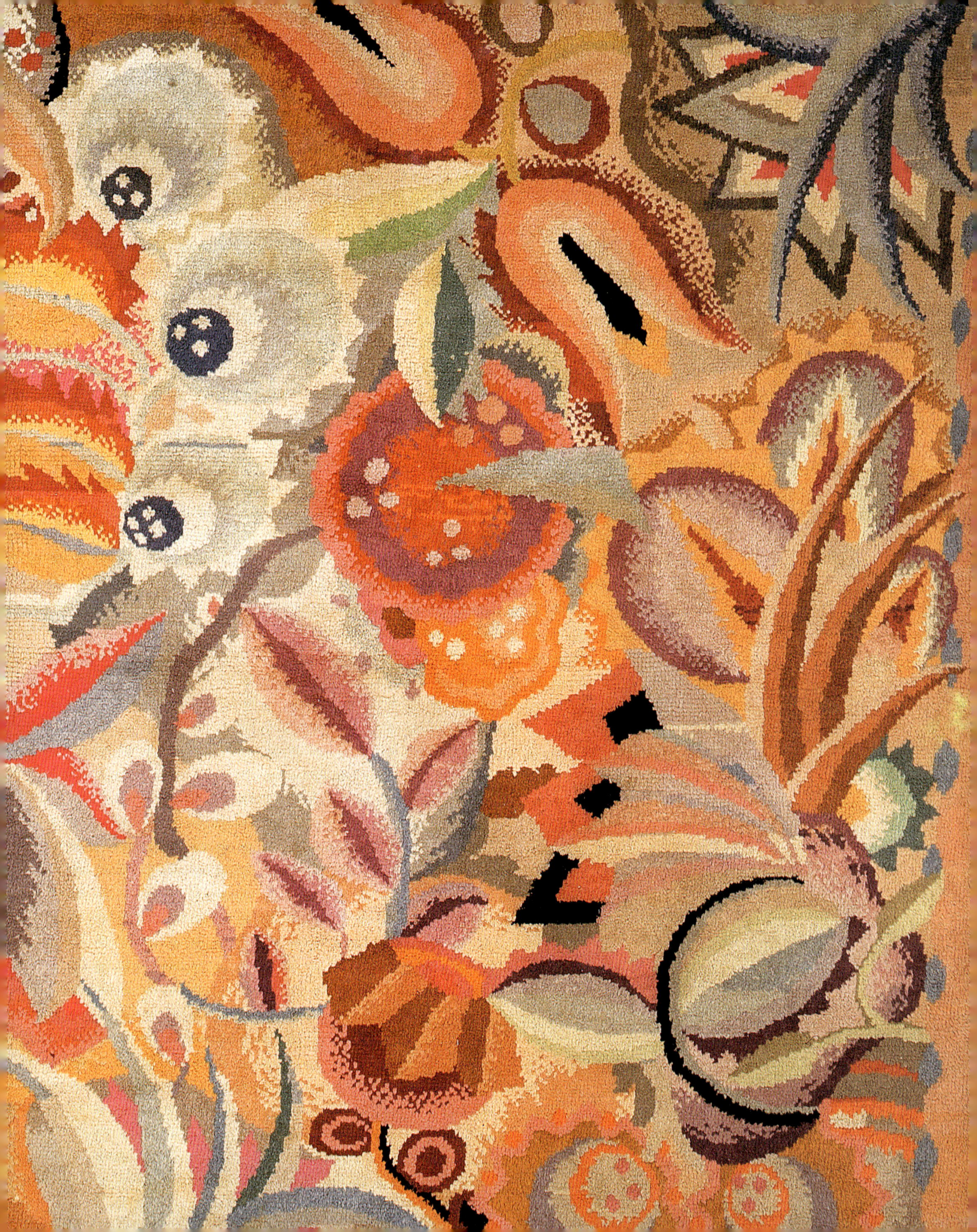

August – September

WEEK 36

MONDAY
31 Holiday, UK exc Scotland

TUESDAY
1

WEDNESDAY
2

THURSDAY
3

T	W	T	F	S	S	M	T	W	T	F	S	S	M		T	W	T	F	S	S	M	T	W	T	F	S	S	M
18	19	20	21	22	23	24	25	26	27	28	29	30	31		1	2	3	4	5	6	7	8	9	10	11	12	13	14

August – September

FRIDAY
4

Holiday, China

SATURDAY
5

○   SUNDAY
6

In Kerman, in the 1890s, madder roots, grape juice, shell fish, indigo, buckthorn, cochineal, onion skins, husk of green walnuts, milk, turmeric, henna, larkspur, and mulberry were all used either singly or in combination to produce the lasting and beautiful shades.

September

WEEK 37

MONDAY
7

Holiday, USA & Canada

TUESDAY
8

WEDNESDAY
9

THURSDAY
10

T	W	T	F	S	S	M	T	W	T	F	S	S	M	T	W	T	F	S	S	M	T	W	T	F	S	S	M	T	W
1	2	3	4	5	6	7	8	9	10	11	12	13	14	15	16	17	18	19	20	21	22	23	24	25	26	27	28	29	30

September

FRIDAY
11

SATURDAY
12

SUNDAY
13

Detail of a hand-woven rug by Hilde Wagner-Ascher made in Austria c. 1925.

T17-1988

SEPTEMBER

WEEK 38

MONDAY
14

TUESDAY
15

HOLIDAY, JAPAN

WEDNESDAY
16

THURSDAY
17

T	W	T	F	S	S	M	T	W	T	F	S	S	M	T	W	T	F	S	S	M	T	W	T	F	S	S	M	T	W
1	2	3	4	5	6	7	8	9	10	11	12	13	14	15	16	17	18	19	20	21	22	23	24	25	26	27	28	29	30

September

FRIDAY
18

SATURDAY
19

SUNDAY
20

The tendency of some synthetic dyes to fade brought oriental carpets into disrepute, and in 1882 laws were passed in Persia to ban the import of aniline dyes and to empower officials to seize and destroy all fabric in which they had been used. If a dyer used them he could have his right hand cut off . . . Some say this prohibition was effective, but others suggest that large quantities of the forbidden dyes were smuggled into Persia and that the law was never strictly enforced.

September

WEEK 39

MONDAY
21

JEWISH NEW YEAR (ROSH HASHANAH)

TUESDAY
22

WEDNESDAY
23

AUTUMNAL EQUINOX, AUTUMN BEGINS   HOLIDAY, JAPAN

THURSDAY
24

T	W	T	F	S	S	M	T	W	T	F	S	S	M	T	W	T	F	S	S	M	T	W	T	F	S	S	M	T	W
1	2	3	4	5	6	7	8	9	10	11	12	13	14	15	16	17	18	19	20	21	22	23	24	25	26	27	28	29	30

September

FRIDAY
25

SATURDAY
26

SUNDAY
27

A late 18th- or 19th-century Caucasian carpet
from Azerbaijan.

330-1892

September – October

WEEK 40

MONDAY
28

TUESDAY
29

WEDNESDAY
30

Day of Atonement (Yom Kippur)

THURSDAY
1

Holiday, China

T	F	S	S	M	T	W	T	F	S	S	M	T	W
17	18	19	20	21	22	23	24	25	26	27	28	29	30

T	F	S	S	M	T	W	T	F	S	S	M	T	W
1	2	3	4	5	6	7	8	9	10	11	12	13	14

September – October

FRIDAY
2

SATURDAY
3

Holiday, Germany

SUNDAY
4

Most weavers can tie between 2,500 and 3,000 knots per day and a good weaver can tie between 6,000 and 10,000 per day. The speed depends not only on the dexterity of the weaver, but on the density of the knots and the nature of the material. it is said that the weavers at the Hereké workshops in Turkey tie 30 knots per minute, which is 14,400 per day.

Overleaf: A hand-knotted carpet designed by Betty Joel and woven in Tientsin, China in 1935–37.

T.296-1977

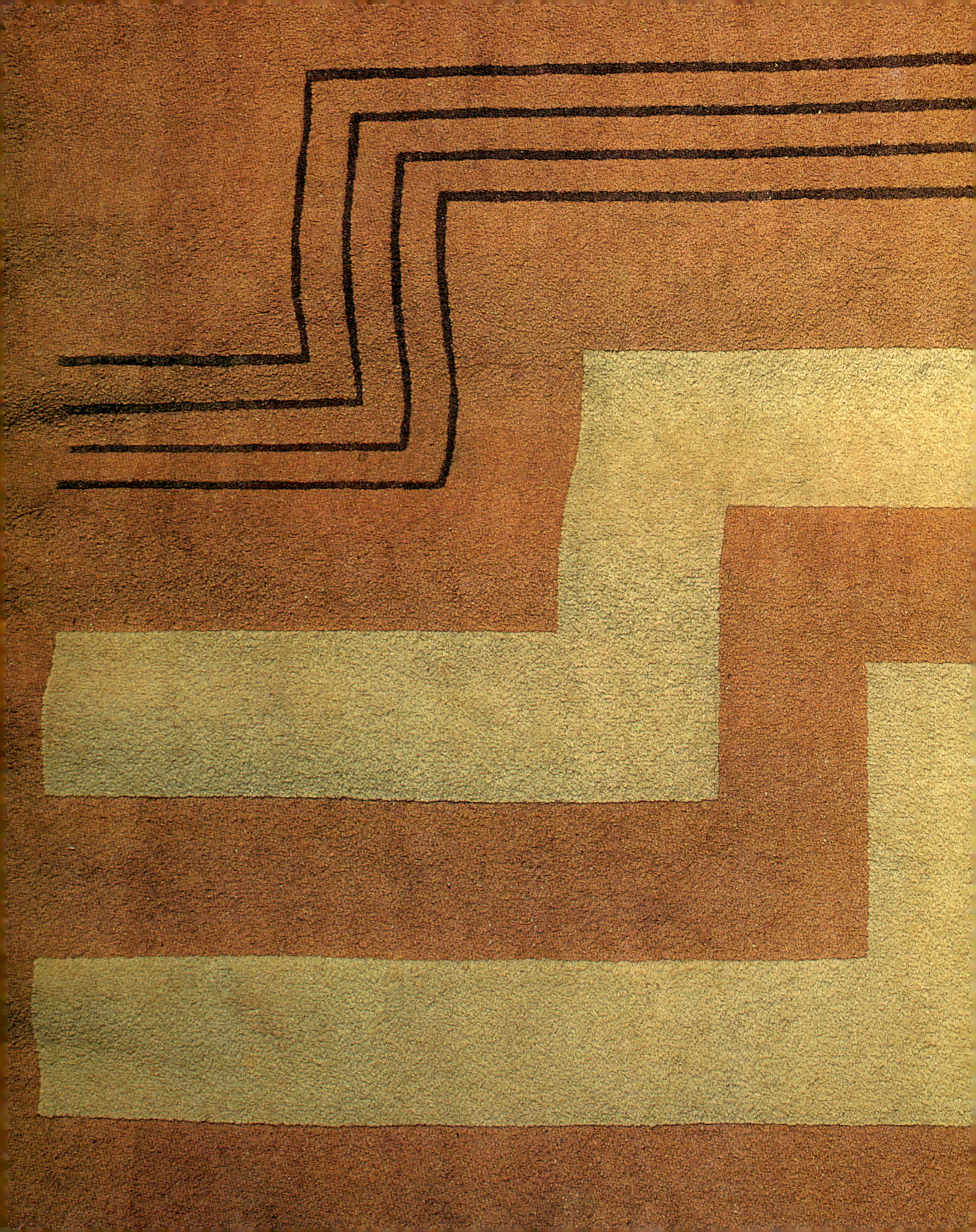

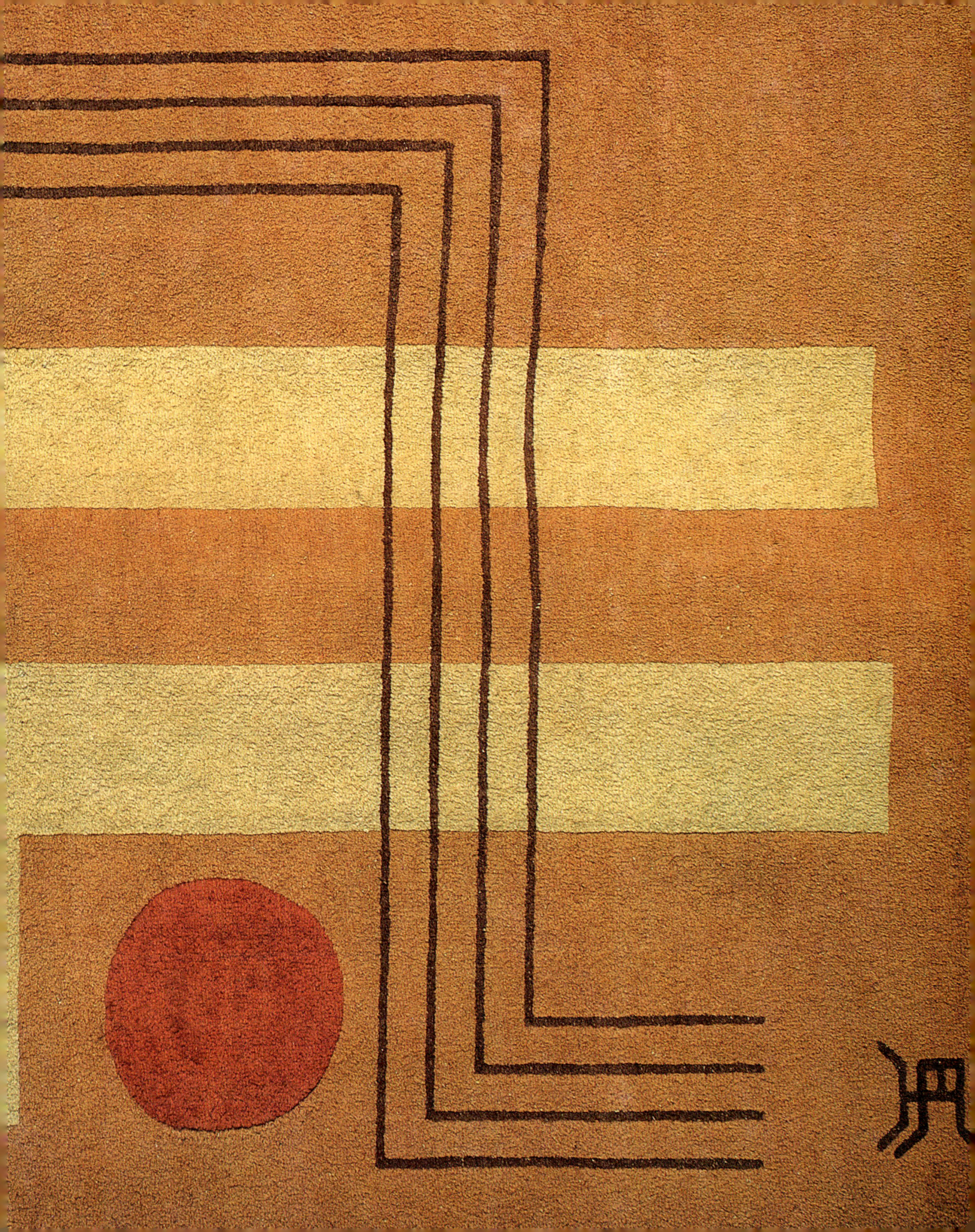

October

WEEK 41

MONDAY
5

○ First day of Tabernacles (Succoth)

TUESDAY
6

WEDNESDAY
7

THURSDAY
8

OCTOBER

FRIDAY
9

HOLIDAY, JAPAN

SATURDAY
10

SUNDAY
11

From about the 1870s onwards, carpets for export were sometimes put into glaring sunlight – or even thrown under the feet of passers-by or under the wheels of vehicles – to modify crude or vivid colours. 'It is no uncommon thing for a new carpet to be laid down in the bazaar for men and animals to trample over it, its owner affirming that this apparently drastic process brings up the pile and enhances the colours.'

Ella C Sykes, *Persia and its People*, London, 1910.

October

WEEK 42

MONDAY
12

◐ Holiday, USA & Canada

TUESDAY
13

WEDNESDAY
14

THURSDAY
15

T	F	S	S	M	T	W	T	F	S	S	M	T	W	T	F	S	S	M	T	W	T	F	S	S	M	T	W	T	F	S
1	2	3	4	5	6	7	8	9	10	11	12	13	14	15	16	17	18	19	20	21	22	23	24	25	26	27	28	29	30	31

October

FRIDAY
16

SATURDAY
17

SUNDAY
18

George Kingman carpet design with flower and leaf motifs.
Worked in the second half of the 19th century.

E554(34)-1956

October

WEEK 43

MONDAY
19

TUESDAY
20   ●

WEDNESDAY
21

THURSDAY
22

October

FRIDAY
23

SATURDAY
24

British Summer Time ends, UK
DST ends, USA

SUNDAY
25

When numbered pieces of toast and marmalade were dropped on various samples of carpet arranged in quality, from coir matting to the finest Kerman rugs, the marmalade-downwards-incidence varied indirectly with the quality of the carpet – the Principle of the Graduated Hostility of Things.

Paul Jennings, *Even Oddlier 'Developments in Resistentialism'*, n.d.

Overleaf: Detail from the corner of a mid-19th century Kurdistan carpet from Persia.
390-1880

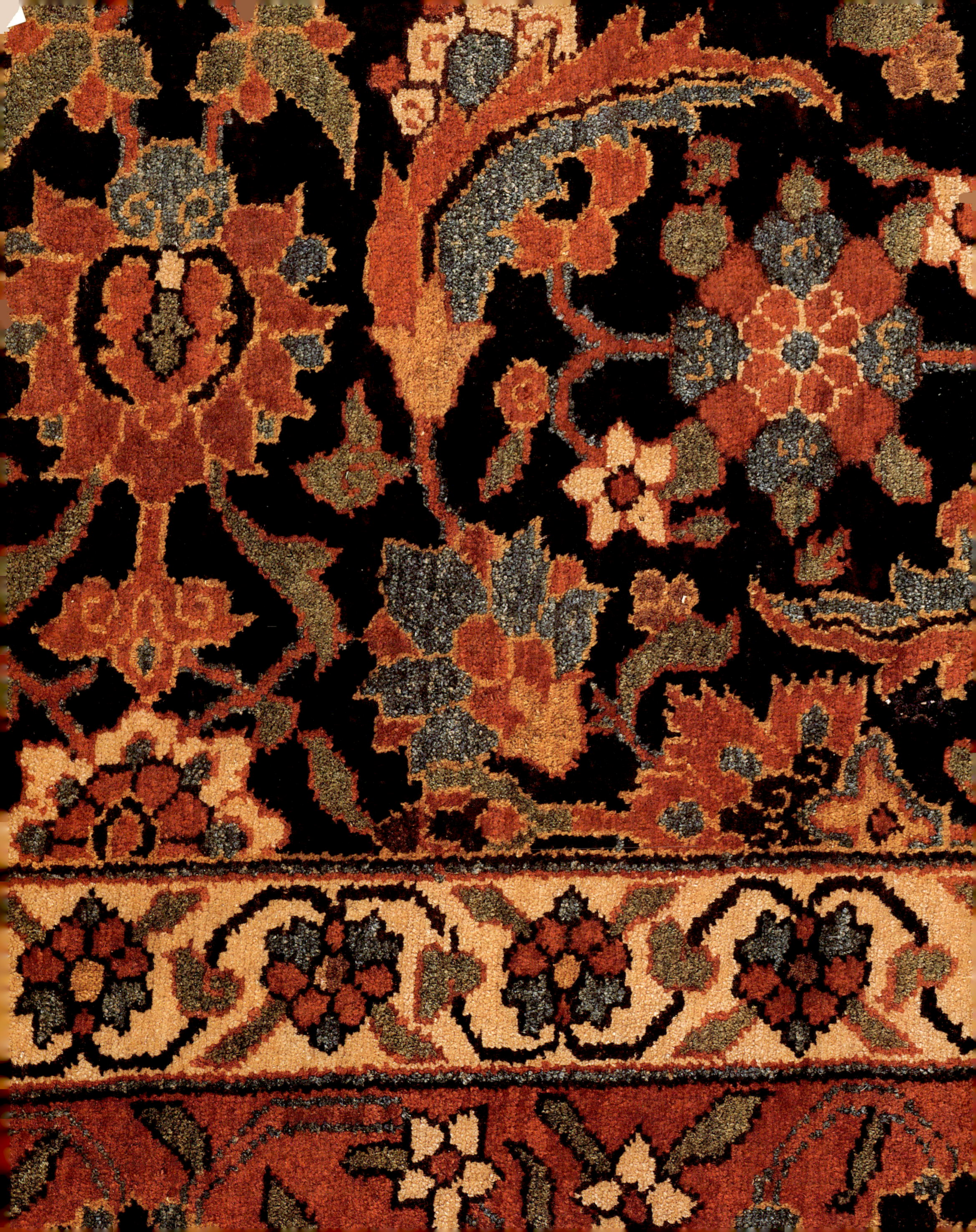

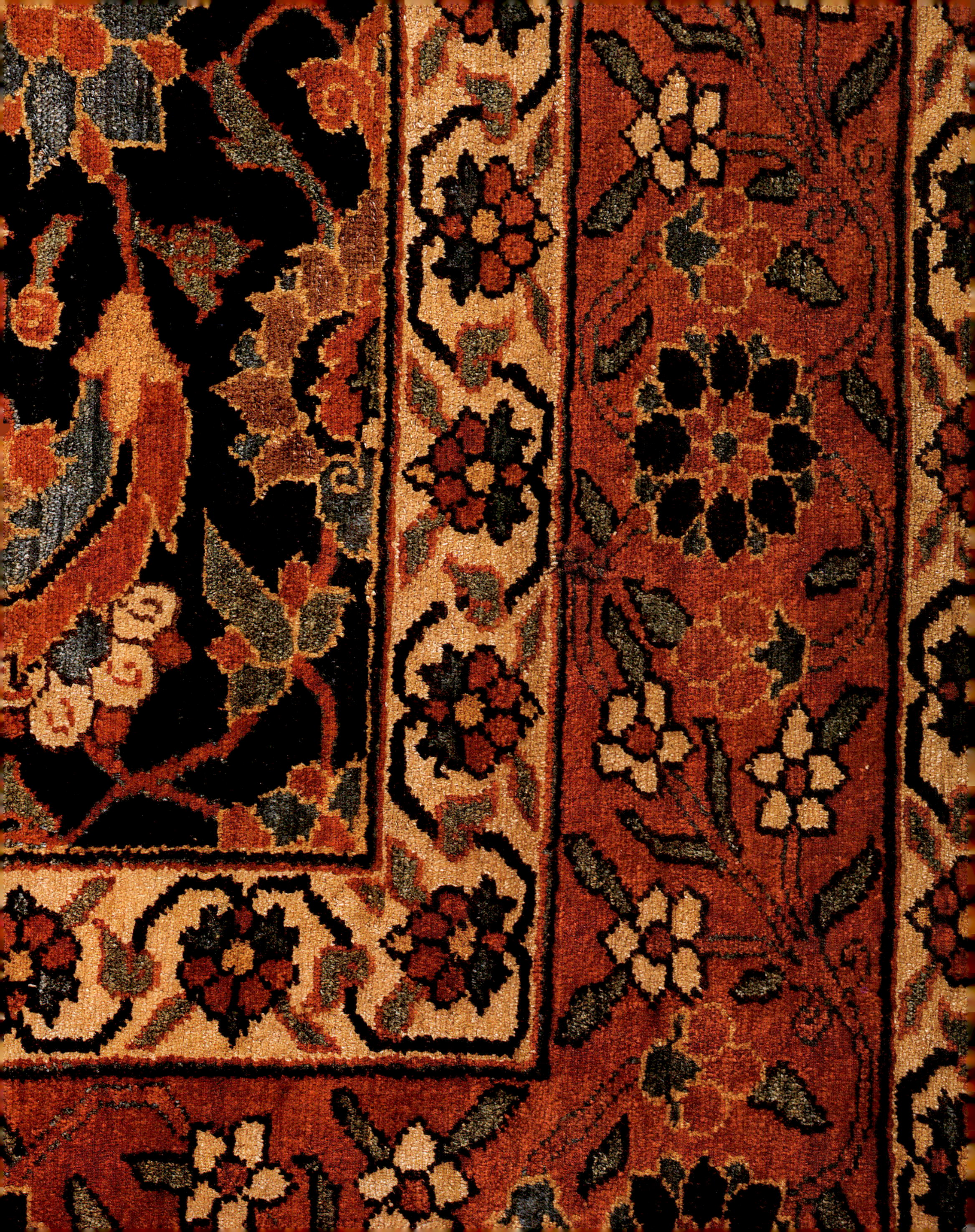

October – November

WEEK 44

MONDAY
26

Holiday, New Zealand

TUESDAY
27

WEDNESDAY
28 ◐

THURSDAY
29

S	S	M	T	W	T	F	S	S	M	T	W	T	F		S	S	M	T	W	T	F	S	S	M	T	W	T	F
17	18	19	20	21	22	23	24	25	26	27	28	29	30		1	2	3	4	5	6	7	8	9	10	11	12	13	14

October – November

FRIDAY
30

SATURDAY
31

ALL SAINTS DAY **SUNDAY**
1

Then came the dust, which fell upon
the Carpet, drifting among the hairs, taking root
in the long deep shadows. More came,
tumbling slowly and with silence
among the waiting hairs,
until the dust thick in the Carpet . . .

Terry Pratchett, *The Carpet People*, 1971, revised 1992.

November

WEEK 45

MONDAY
2

TUESDAY   Holiday, Japan
3

WEDNESDAY   ○
4

THURSDAY
5

S	M	T	W	T	F	S	S	M	T	W	T	F	S	S	M	T	W	T	F	S	S	M	T	W	T	F	S	S	M
1	2	3	4	5	6	7	8	9	10	11	12	13	14	15	16	17	18	19	20	21	22	23	24	25	26	27	28	29	30

November

FRIDAY
6

SATURDAY
7

Remembrance Sunday

SUNDAY
8

A rug designed by Vanessa Bell and hand-knotted on canvas in 1914 for the Omega Workshops, London.
CIRC.660-1962

November

WEEK 46

MONDAY
9

TUESDAY
10

WEDNESDAY
11
◐ Holiday, USA, Canada & France

THURSDAY
12

S	M	T	W	T	F	S	S	M	T	W	T	F	S	S	M	T	W	T	F	S	S	M	T	W	T	F	S	S	M
1	2	3	4	5	6	7	8	9	10	11	12	13	14	15	16	17	18	19	20	21	22	23	24	25	26	27	28	29	30

November

FRIDAY
13

Birthday of the Prince of Wales

SATURDAY
14

SUNDAY
15

In the English-speaking world the word rug (from related Old Norse, Norwegian, and Swedish words for a type of coarse, shaggy, wool bed covering) was used throughout the nineteenth century for a bed covering, often termed bed rug or bed rugg.

Sarah B. Sherill, *Carpets and Rugs of Europe and America*, London, 1995.

November

WEEK 47

MONDAY
16

TUESDAY
17

WEDNESDAY
18

THURSDAY
19   ●

S	M	T	W	T	F	S	S	M	T	W	T	F	S	S	M	T	W	T	F	S	S	M	T	W	T	F	S	S	M
1	2	3	4	5	6	7	8	9	10	11	12	13	14	15	16	17	18	19	20	21	22	23	24	25	26	27	28	29	30

November

FRIDAY
20

SATURDAY
21

SUNDAY
22

A ryijy rug from Finland, dated 1799.
T.8-1914

November

WEEK 48

MONDAY   Holiday, Japan
23

TUESDAY
24

WEDNESDAY
25

THURSDAY   Holiday, USA
26

S	M	T	W	T	F	S	S	M	T	W	T	F	S	S	M	T	W	T	F	S	S	M	T	W	T	F	S	S	M
1	2	3	4	5	6	7	8	9	10	11	12	13	14	15	16	17	18	19	20	21	22	23	24	25	26	27	28	29	30

November

FRIDAY
27

SATURDAY
28

FIRST SUNDAY IN ADVENT   SUNDAY
29

In carpets, English manufacturers make a very distinguished display, though the most essential feature, aesthetically, is uniformly disregarded, namely that a carpet is made to be trodden upon . . . The great feature required of a carpet is that it express flatness.

'Art Moderne Rugs from France', in *Good Furniture Magazine*, February 1928.

Overleaf: Detail from the centre of a carpet designed and hand-knotted in England by Jean Milne c. 1945.
CIRC.315-1961

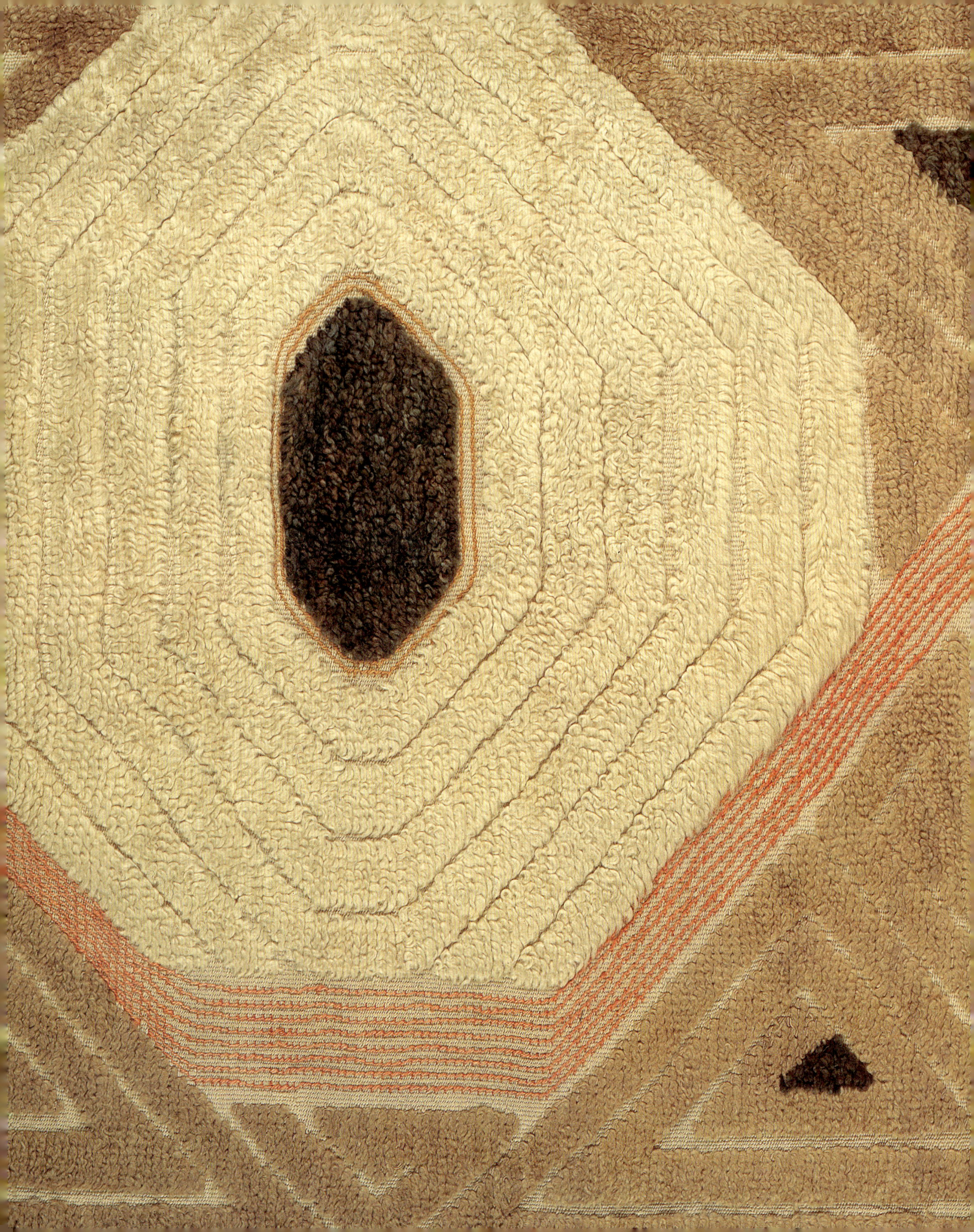

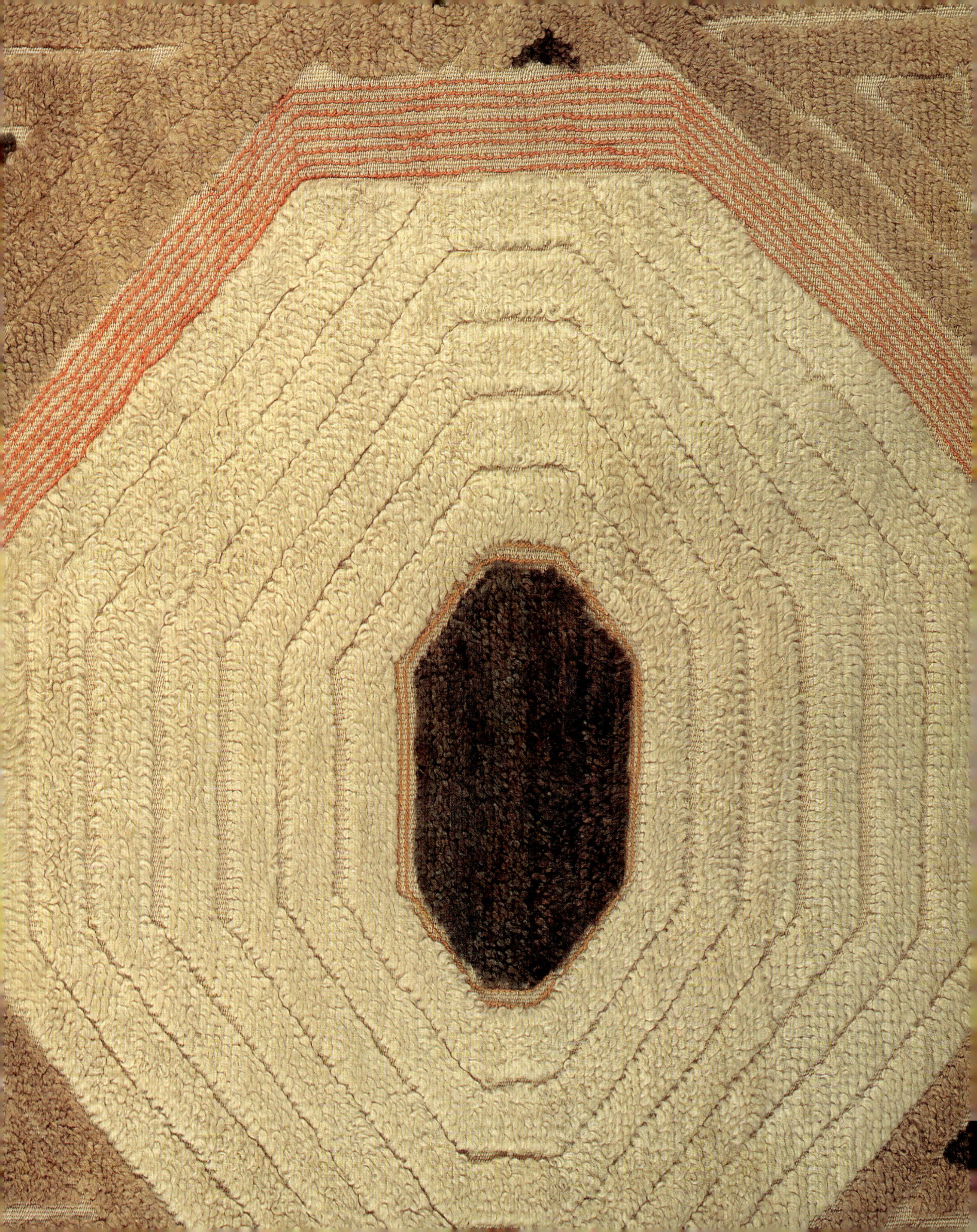

November – December

WEEK 49

MONDAY   St. Andrew's Day
30

TUESDAY
1

WEDNESDAY
2

THURSDAY   ○
3

T	W	T	F	S	S	M	T	W	T	F	S	S	M		T	W	T	F	S	S	M	T	W	T	F	S	S	M
17	18	19	20	21	22	23	24	25	26	27	28	29	30		1	2	3	4	5	6	7	8	9	10	11	12	13	14

November – December

FRIDAY
4

SATURDAY
5

SUNDAY
6

The President wishes to get a Carpet of the best Kind, for a Room 32 feet by 22 . . . We can get no Carpet in New York to suit the Room . . . If you will be so good as to inform me if anything of the above description can be found in Philadelphia you will oblige me.

Tobias Lear to Clement Biddle, 10 February 1790.

December

WEEK 50

MONDAY
7

TUESDAY
8

Holiday, Italy

WEDNESDAY
9

THURSDAY
10

◐

| T | W | T | F | S | S | M | T | W | T | F | S | S | M | T | W | T | F | S | S | M | T | W | T | F | S | S | M | T | W | T |
|1|2|3|4|5|6|7|8|9|10|11|12|13|14|15|16|17|18|19|20|21|22|23|24|25|26|27|28|29|30|31|

December

FRIDAY
11

SATURDAY
12

SUNDAY
13

A detail from the Chelsea Carpet, an early
16th-century Persian carpet which gets its name from
the fact it was bought from a dealer in the King's Road,
Chelsea, London.

589-1890

December

WEEK 51

MONDAY
14

TUESDAY
15

WEDNESDAY
16

THURSDAY
17

T	W	T	F	S	S	M	T	W	T	F	S	S	M	T	W	T	F	S	S	M	T	W	T	F	S	S	M	T	W	T
1	2	3	4	5	6	7	8	9	10	11	12	13	14	15	16	17	18	19	20	21	22	23	24	25	26	27	28	29	30	31

December

FRIDAY
18

SATURDAY
19

FIRST DAY OF RAMADAN

SUNDAY
20

When Eleanor of Castile arrived in London in 1255 to marry Prince Edward, she brought with her carpets from Spain to decorate her rooms in Westminster. Such an ostentatious display of wealth made her the target of much criticism.

December

WEEK 52

MONDAY
21

TUESDAY
22

Winter Solstice, Winter begins

WEDNESDAY
23

Holiday, Japan

THURSDAY
24

Christmas Eve

December

CHRISTMAS DAY

FRIDAY
25

◑ BOXING DAY

SATURDAY
26

SUNDAY
27

A sample of machine-woven Brussels carpeting woven in about 1855.

December – January 1999

MONDAY
28
Holiday, UK

TUESDAY
29

WEDNESDAY
30

THURSDAY
31

F	S	S	M	T	W	T	F	S	S	M	T	W	T		F	S	S	M	T	W	T	F	S	S	M	T	W	T
18	19	20	21	22	23	24	25	26	27	28	29	30	31		1	2	3	4	5	6	7	8	9	10	11	12	13	14

December – January 1999

HOLIDAY, NEW YEAR'S DAY

FRIDAY

1

HOLIDAY, SCOTLAND (TBC)

SATURDAY

2

SUNDAY

3

As the fashionable 'modernistic' interior became increasingly streamlined with walls and upholsteries in neutral shades . . . rugs with striking abstract patterns in assertive colours were sought after by the affluent minority to provide focal points and decorative relief.

Valerie Mendes, *Thirties*, London, 1979, p. 87.

Forward Planner

JANUARY

FEBRUARY

MARCH

APRIL

MAY

JUNE

JULY

AUGUST

SEPTEMBER

OCTOBER

NOVEMBER

DECEMBER

Notes

Notes

Notes

Addresses

Name	Name
Address	Address
Tel: Fax:	Tel: Fax:
Name	Name
Address	Address
Tel: Fax:	Tel: Fax:
Name	Name
Address	Address
Tel: Fax:	Tel: Fax:
Name	Name
Address	Address
Tel: Fax:	Tel: Fax:
Name	Name
Address	Address
Tel: Fax:	Tel: Fax:
Name	Name
Address	Address
Tel: Fax:	Tel: Fax:
Name	Name
Address	Address
Tel: Fax:	Tel: Fax:
Name	Name
Address	Address
Tel: Fax:	Tel: Fax:
Name	Name
Address	Address
Tel: Fax:	Tel: Fax:

| Name |
| Address |
| Tel: Fax: |

| Name |
| Address |
| Tel: Fax: |

| Name |
| Address |
| Tel: Fax: |

| Name |
| Address |
| Tel: Fax: |

| Name |
| Address |
| Tel: Fax: |

| Name |
| Address |
| Tel: Fax: |

| Name |
| Address |
| Tel: Fax: |

| Name |
| Address |
| Tel: Fax: |

| Name |
| Address |
| Tel: Fax: |

| Name |
| Address |
| Tel: Fax: |

| Name |
| Address |
| Tel: Fax: |

| Name |
| Address |
| Tel: Fax: |

| Name |
| Address |
| Tel: Fax: |

| Name |
| Address |
| Tel: Fax: |

| Name |
| Address |
| Tel: Fax: |

| Name |
| Address |
| Tel: Fax: |

| Name |
| Address |
| Tel: Fax: |

| Name |
| Address |
| Tel: Fax: |

| Name |
| Address |
| Tel: Fax: |

| Name |
| Address |
| Tel: Fax: |

Name		Name	
Address		Address	
Tel:	Fax:	Tel:	Fax:
Name		Name	
Address		Address	
Tel:	Fax:	Tel:	Fax:
Name		Name	
Address		Address	
Tel:	Fax:	Tel:	Fax:
Name		Name	
Address		Address	
Tel:	Fax:	Tel:	Fax:
Name		Name	
Address		Address	
Tel:	Fax:	Tel:	Fax:
Name		Name	
Address		Address	
Tel:	Fax:	Tel:	Fax:
Name		Name	
Address		Address	
Tel:	Fax:	Tel:	Fax:
Name		Name	
Address		Address	
Tel:	Fax:	Tel:	Fax:
Name		Name	
Address		Address	
Tel:	Fax:	Tel:	Fax:
Name		Name	
Address		Address	
Tel:	Fax:	Tel:	Fax:

Name			Name		
Address			Address		
Tel:		Fax:	Tel:		Fax:

Name			Name		
Address			Address		
Tel:		Fax:	Tel:		Fax:

Name			Name		
Address			Address		
Tel:		Fax:	Tel:		Fax:

Name			Name		
Address			Address		
Tel:		Fax:	Tel:		Fax:

Name			Name		
Address			Address		
Tel:		Fax:	Tel:		Fax:

Name			Name		
Address			Address		
Tel:		Fax:	Tel:		Fax:

Name			Name		
Address			Address		
Tel:		Fax:	Tel:		Fax:

Name			Name		
Address			Address		
Tel:		Fax:	Tel:		Fax:

Name			Name		
Address			Address		
Tel:		Fax:	Tel:		Fax:

Name			Name		
Address			Address		
Tel:		Fax:	Tel:		Fax:

Name		Name	
Address		Address	
Tel:	Fax:	Tel:	Fax:
Name		Name	
Address		Address	
Tel:	Fax:	Tel:	Fax:
Name		Name	
Address		Address	
Tel:	Fax:	Tel:	Fax:
Name		Name	
Address		Address	
Tel:	Fax:	Tel:	Fax:
Name		Name	
Address		Address	
Tel:	Fax:	Tel:	Fax:
Name		Name	
Address		Address	
Tel:	Fax:	Tel:	Fax:
Name		Name	
Address		Address	
Tel:	Fax:	Tel:	Fax:
Name		Name	
Address		Address	
Tel:	Fax:	Tel:	Fax:
Name		Name	
Address		Address	
Tel:	Fax:	Tel:	Fax:
Name		Name	
Address		Address	
Tel:	Fax:	Tel:	Fax: